Reasons Book 1

Got Questions?

We Have
*Reasons for Hope**

Shari S. Abbott

This book is dedicated
to the Wednesday morning ladies,
who reason together from the Scriptures.

&

to the One whose reasons
give us true hope and real joy.

To Him alone be all honor and glory.

Got Questions?
We Have *Reasons for Hope*

Reasons Book 1

That I may publish with the voice of thanksgiving, and tell of all thy wondrous works. (Psalm 26:7)

Published by Psalm267 Publishing
www.psalm267.com

Edited by Rosemary Stein.

Cover design by Tamara Schmitz.

All emphasis and bracketed information added.

Printed in the United States of America

ISBN: 978-0-9885513-4-3

Contents

Sanctify the Lord God in your hearts:
and be ready always to give an answer
to every man that asketh you a
*reason of the hope**
that is in you with meekness and fear
1 Peter 3:15

Come now, and let us
reason together...
Isaiah 1:18

This hope we have as an anchor of the soul,
both sure and steadfast...
Hebrews 6:19

FOREWORD

Sir Winston Churchill (1874-1965) famously said, "Men occasionally stumble over the truth, but most of them pick themselves up and hurry off as if nothing ever happened." Such is the spirit of our times. Facts are twisted (if not totally replaced) with "spin" and politically-correct "nuancing." Belief in universally applicable absolute truths has long since been abandoned in favor of subjectivism. If Churchill were alive today it is likely that his oft-repeated lament over man's aversion to truth would be voiced much more strongly.

But the cultural soul of the West was not always this way. There was a time when truth seriously mattered. America and Europe were built on truth, because the cultures were rooted in Christianity. Long before Charles, Prince of Wales (whose title includes the phrase, "Defender of the Faith") would cheat on his wife and dedicate Buddhist temples, long before John Lennon would convince adoring fans that "nothing is real" and "the Beatles are bigger than Jesus," and centuries prior to the loss of God insisted on by Darwinism, there was a time when even theological truths mattered. I bring up the progression away from truth that happened in Europe and Britain because it preceded (and greatly contributed to) the loss of truth that would eventually corrupt America.

But it might be encouraging to look back at a time when truth mattered so much that even politicians were careful to speak with utmost theological precision. When concern arose among Britain's Parliament that government and church were in danger of influence from unbiblical and unwholesome teachings, officials acted to keep culture and legislature focused on truth (with God's word being truth's ultimate foundation). In June of 1643 Parliament passed an act called (take a deep breath before reading further), "An Ordinance of the Lords and Commons in Parliament for the Calling an Assembly of learned and godly divines and others, to be consulted with by the Parliament, for the settlement of the Government and Liturgy of the Church of England, and for the indicating and cleaning of the doctrine of the said Church from false aspersions and interpretations." Whew! The quest for truth was important enough that an act of Parliament—with a 60 word title, no less—was ratified to ensure its preservation.

Fast forward to the 21st-century when both church and culture have drifted in ways that would have left our Christian ancestors horrified. United Methodist pastors endorse a syncretistic meshing of Bible and Koran called "Chrislam." The Presbyterian Church USA is on record affirming abortion, gay marriage, and the ordination of homosexual clergy. Historically Baptist schools (like Furman and Meredith) won't allow speakers on campus who affirm the Biblical account of creation, or who say that Jesus is the One and only Savior.

President Obama—who campaigned with a promise to defend traditional marriage—got to the Oval Office with the help of gay activist money, only to announce that his views on human sexuality had "evolved." Even the most diligent Christian parents must be discouraged to know that their children will get many times more hours of content from radically secular classrooms and hedonistic media then they ever will from church and youth group.

~~~

Such realities make the scholarship and ministry of a person like Shari Abbott all the more relevant. In every age God raises up leaders—voices of truth and bearers of light—and Shari is one for our times. It has been my privilege to read Shari Abbott's writing for several years now. She has a solid grasp on biblical truth, great skill as an apologist, plus the ability to engage the reader through stories and personal application. I have come to trust her as a
~~~

meticulous Christian thinker who has discernment that clearly comes from the Holy Spirit. My prayer is that her platform as a writer will grow and be used by the Lord for many years!

In the fight for truth, there is hope! Time and again, God has equipped members of His body to sow the seeds of truth in the hearts and minds of their generation. Shari Abbott is one in our times who accurately and artfully proclaims truth. I commend to you this, her latest work.

Few from Churchill's time could have foreseen the rapid decline of truth that would characterize the 1970's-present (he died in the 1960's). But if those of Churchill's generation could somehow have glimpsed the godlessness of the 21st century, I am convinced that they would have pushed harder for preemptive measures to counter the slide.

We can't go back in time and undo the past. But for God and country, for the sake of future generations who will come after us, we can start to proclaim and defend truth…now. May we not look back one day and ponder what we should have done! I thank the Lord for gifted, industrious Christians like Shari Abbott who create resources like this book—for all who care about truth.

Dr. Alex McFarland
Director, Apologetics and Christian Worldview
North Greenville University, SC
June, 2014

PREFACE

What is apologetics and why should I care?

Apologetics is a branch of theology that offers a defense of Christian doctrine. It is practiced by Christians when we give reasoned answers (reasoned from Scripture) for what we believe.

Reasons for Hope*Jesus is a 501c3 Christian apologetics ministry. It is our mission to equip Christians with reasoned answers from the Bible so they are able to stand firm on what they believe and are empowered to share what they believe. Our ministry is founded on the words of Peter in 1 Peter 3:15

> *Sanctify the Lord God in your hearts: and be ready always to give an* ***answer*** [apologia] *to every man that asketh you a* *reason* *of the hope that is in you with meekness and fear.*

In this verse we see two important words. The word answer in English Bibles is a translation of the Greek word apologia from which we get the word apologetics. The Strong's Dictionary defines apologia as:

> *apologia, ap-ol-og-ee'-ah; from the same as G626; a plea ("apology"):--****answer*** *(for self), clearing of self,* ***defense.***

Note also that the Greek word **apologia** is defined as a **defense**. From this we are instructed to defend the Word of God. That is done by giving reasoned answers. The foundation of our faith and the reasons and answers for what we believe have been graciously revealed to us by God through His Word.

In 1 Peter 3:15 we also find the word **reason.** We are told to give a **reason** for the hope we have in us.

> *Sanctify the Lord God in your hearts: and be ready always to give an* ***answer*** [apologia] *to every man that asketh you a* *reason* [logos] *of the hope that is in you with meekness and fear:*

Reason is the English translation of the Greek word logos, which is also translated as "word." The Strong's Dictionary defines logos as:

> *logos, log'-os; from G3004; something said (including the thought); by impl. a topic (subject of discourse), also* ***reasoning*** *(the mental faculty) or motive. . . account, cause, communication. . . doctrine, fame. . .intent, matter, mouth, preaching, question,* ***reason, + reckon****, remove, say (-ing), shew. . .speech, talk. . .tidings, treatise, utterance, word, work.*

In the more precise Greek language we learn a fine distinction about the importance of reasoning. As defined by Strong's Dictionary, reasoning is thoughtful study and mental evaluation of subject matter and discourses and the word denotes sharing information (tidings) by communication through speaking (speech, talk, utterance, word), writing (treatise) and/or showing (shew, work).

As Christians we have the presence and power of the Holy Spirit indwelling us to lead, teach, guide and grow us (John 15:26, John 16:13). Therefore we are able to reason from the Scriptures to know, understand and share our Hope.

Why should we care?

Why should we study apologetics?

Because we have been commissioned and commanded to understand God's Word so we can live and share what we know.

Whether we are speaking to believers or non-believers about what we believe, or whether we are writing about or showing our faith by our actions, we proclaim Christ's name until He comes.

At Reasons for Hope*Jesus we approach the Word of God and spiritual growth with a three-fold method of **Know it! Live it! Share it!**

Jesus commissioned and commanded us to know, live and share what we believe:

Know it!

Reasoning, studying and
evaluating what we believe.

Herein is my Father glorified,
that ye bear much fruit;
so shall ye be my ***disciples****.*
(John 15:8)

Live it!

Showing what we believe.

Let your light so shine before men,
that they may see your ***good works****,*
and glorify your Father which is in heaven.
(Matthew 5:16)

Share it!

Speaking/writing about what we believe.

And [Jesus] *said unto them,*
Go ye into all the world, and
preach the gospel *to every creature.*

(Mark 16:15)

Paul and Peter also spoke of the importance of giving reasoned answers for what we believe. In his letters we find the same commission that Jesus gave—to know, live and share what we believe.

Know it!

Reasoning, studying and
evaluating what we believe.

<u>Study</u> *to show thyself approved unto God,*
a workman that needeth not to be ashamed,
rightly dividing the word of truth.
(2 Timothy 2:15)

Live it!

Showing what we believe.

For so hath the Lord commanded us, saying,
I have set thee to ***<u>be a light</u>*** *of the Gentiles,*
that thou shouldest be for salvation
unto the ends of the earth.
(Acts 13:47)

Share it!

Speaking/writing about what we believe.

And he [Jesus] *commanded us*
to ***<u>preach</u>*** *unto the people,*
and to ***<u>testify</u>*** *that it is he* [Jesus]
which was ordained of God to be
the Judge of quick and dead.
(Acts 10:42)

This brings us back to where we started. What is apologetics? Peter answered that question with his exhortation to all who know and love Jesus:

Sanctify the Lord God in your hearts:
and be ready always to give an answer
to every man that asketh you a reason of the hope
that is in you with meekness and fear (1 Peter 3:15)

Grow in faith—Know it! Live it! Share it!

At Reasons for Hope*Jesus we work to equip Christians with reasoned answers so they will be ready always to know, live and share what they believe. That's what the Reasons Books are all about.

Got Questions?

The Word of God has

Reasons for Hope.

All Christians need to be prepared through reasoning, studying and evaluating (Know it!). We need to communicate what we believe by showing, speaking and writing about our faith (Live it! and Share it!).

Go forth as Christ commissioned and commanded and do so "with meekness and fear." That means with kindness and gentleness be diligent and "fervent in spirit, serving the Lord"(Romans 12:11).

All truth is given by revelation, either general or special, and it must be received by reason. ***Reason*** *is the God-given means for discovering the truth that God discloses, whether in his world or his Word. While God wants to reach the heart with truth, he does not bypass the mind.* *— Jonathan Edwards*

INTRODUCTION

Reasons Book #1

Everyone has questions! We all have questions and we all want answers.

The world around us is growing more challenging and confusing with each passing day. We live in a time when knowledge is increasing greatly, so we must ask, "is wisdom increasing also?" Truth is being redefined and morals and ethics are becoming situational rather than absolute. For many people there is no standard, but for Christians we have a standard by which to live—God's Word.

As Christians we must challenge ourselves with the questions, what do I believe and why do I believe what I believe?

As Christians we have a Book that gives us all the answers—the Holy Bible. In the words of the Bible we find true wisdom that comes from absolute truth—from the only One who is Truth.

The Bible

It has been said that the word Bible can be thought of as an acronym for:

Basic
Instructions
Before
Leaving
Earth

The Bible is our instruction book. It is our guide for everyday life, because it reveals the only One who lived a perfectly righteous life, and therefore it should be read daily. When we pray, we speak to God; and when we read the Bible, He speaks to us.

Regular Bible reading will generate lots of questions, as we try to understand the mind, the will and the ways of our God. Questions are a very good thing. They cause us to dig deeper into God's Word and to consider more carefully the truths found there.

At Reasons for Hope*Jesus we take the Bible both seriously and literally. We know that through diligent study of the Word and careful consideration of the historical context and grammatical style, the Holy Spirit will teach us and guide us in the truths God has given:

> *John 16:13 Howbeit when he, the Spirit of truth, is come, he will guide you into all truth: for he shall not speak of himself; but whatsoever he shall hear, that shall he speak: and he will show you things to come.*

When we encounter difficult Bible passages we must remember that God doesn't expect us to understand everything that He has said. He does, however, expect us to believe *every word* that proceeds from Him:

> *Matthew 4:4 ...Man shall not live by bread alone, but by every word that proceedeth out of the mouth of God.*

Where do these questions come from?

At Reasons for Hope*Jesus we receive a lot of questions each year. We feel honored that people ask us to join them in searching God's Word for truth. This book is a compilation of some of the questions we have received, along with answers and reasons for what we believe God's Word reveals to us.

Note: For Bible verses, all emphasis and bracketed information has been added.

If you are a Christian, you are not a citizen of this world trying to get to heaven; you are a citizen of heaven making your way through this world.

— Vance Havner

Q. 1

Jesus said, "I never knew you." Why would He say that to people who serve Him?

Q. I am a believer and have been a Christian for years. There's one part of the Bible that confuses me though. It's where people say to Jesus that they did many miracles and works in His name, but He says that he never knew them. I thought if you're saved, and if signs and wonders follow you, that it was an indication you have a good relationship with Jesus and that you are bound for Heaven. Who are these miracle-working people who do all these great works only to be rejected as not knowing Jesus? It's almost like I'm reading this out of context.

The verse referred to in this question is Matthew 7:23 and the context of this verse is key to understanding it.

> *Matthew 7:21-23 Not every one that saith unto me, Lord, Lord, shall enter into the kingdom of heaven; but he that doeth the will of my Father which is in heaven. Many will say to me in that day, Lord, Lord, have we not prophesied in thy name? and in thy name have cast out devils? and in thy name done many wonderful works?* ***And then will I profess unto them, I never knew you: depart from me, ye that work iniquity.***

"In that day" is a key phrase that is used throughout the Bible to refer to a future time of judgment—a day when people will stand before God and their eternal destiny will be determined. This judgment will not include those who have been saved during the age of the Holy Spirit, in which we live. As believers, our judgment for our eternal destiny was done at the cross. Our sins were laid upon Jesus and He paid the penalty for them. When we repent and trust in Him, we receive forgiveness for our sins and His righteousness is imputed to us (2 Corinthians 5:21). We also receive eternal life with Him (John 3:16) and the gift of the Holy Spirit to lead and guide us (John 16:13). And, we are sealed by the Holy Spirit (Ephesians 4:30).

The judgment spoken of in Matthew 7 is often referred to as the Great White Throne Judgment, and it is a judgment of works. Remember, nobody does works that are worthy of Heaven—none are righteous, no not one (Romans 3:10). All the good works in the world cannot wipe away the penalty of sin. But as Christians, our sins are paid for by One whose works are perfect and sufficient. The blood of the perfect, righteous Lamb of God has made us worthy of Heaven.

When Jesus spoke these words recorded in Matthew 7:21-23, he had just finished talking about how we can judge false prophets by their fruit (Matthew 7:15-20). The passage is very clear. It speaks of wolves that look like sheep, thorns that look like grapes and thistles that look like figs.

Jesus spoke of the contrast of good, fruitful, trees and corrupt trees with bad fruit:

> *Matthew 7:17-20 Even so every good tree bringeth forth good fruit; but a corrupt tree bringeth forth evil fruit. A good tree cannot bring forth evil fruit, neither can a corrupt tree bring forth good fruit. Every tree that bringeth not forth good fruit is hewn down, and cast into the fire. Wherefore by their fruits ye shall know them.*

Man's "fruits" are his works. So with these words Jesus reminds us that we cannot judge the heart of man, but we can judge his works. Both the profession of faith in Christ and the evidence of the fruits of faith should be apparent in every believer's life. If we don't see good fruit in the life of someone who professes to be a follower of Christ, we should wonder. And that wondering should cause us to share the gospel with them. If their profession is true, hopefully it will call the person to repentance and they will begin to exhibit good "fruit" in their lives. If the person is someone who is not saved, hopefully sharing the gospel will turn their hearts to Christ and they will come to trust in Him.

Let's now consider those in the Matthew 7 passage who have evidence of good fruit but are denied by Jesus. In verse 21 Jesus stated that not everyone who professes to know Him will enter the Kingdom of Heaven—only those who "...do the will of My Father..."

> *Matthew 7:21 Not every one that saith unto me, Lord, Lord, shall enter into the kingdom of heaven; but he that doeth the will of my Father which is in heaven.*

Jesus is saying that doing the will of His Father in Heaven is prerequisite to entering the Kingdom of Heaven. What is the will of the Father? This is revealed in Jesus' obedience to the Father's will. Jesus' mission on earth was to seek and save the lost.

> *Luke 19:10 For the Son of man is come to seek and to save that which was lost.*

Jesus was obedient to the Father's will of restoring mankind to right relationship with God. Jesus lived the perfect life and willingly went to the cross, dying the atoning death that opened the way for forgiveness of sins.

> *The ultimate test of our spirituality is the measure of our amazement at the grace of God. Holiness is not something we are called upon to do in order that we may become something; it is something we are to do because of what we already are.*
>
> — *Martyn Lloyd-Jones*

We know that salvation is the will of the Father. That's why He sent Jesus to earth. Peter tells us that God is *"not willing that any should perish, but that all should come to repentance"* (2 Peter 3:9).

We also know that salvation is a gift *from* the Father *through* the Son. It is by grace alone, through faith that we are saved (Ephesians 2:8). It is freely given to all who repent and trust in the life, death, burial and resurrection of the Lord Jesus Christ.

The Christian does not think that God will love us because we are good, but that God will make us good because He loves us.
— C.S. Lewis

The people spoken of in Matthew 7:22 are those who are numbered in the group Jesus spoke of in verse 21. They will not enter the Kingdom of Heaven because they have not done the Father's will. They have not repented and trusted in Jesus and therefore Jesus does not know them.

You might say, how can we judge their hearts? Well, we aren't judging their hearts. In this passage Jesus judged both their words and their works. Remember, this judgment is future, and in that day they will call upon Jesus as Lord. But on what basis do they know Him? These people give as evidence of their worthiness their own good works that they have done, not Jesus' work willingly done for them and in accordance with the will of the Father. Read how they claim their worth based on their own works:

> *Matthew 7:22 Many will say to me in that day, Lord, Lord, have we not prophesied in thy name? and in thy name have cast out devils? and in thy name done many wonderful works.*

These people are counting on their good works to make them righteous, rather than the righteousness of Jesus which is freely given to all who repent and trust in Him.

These people have not understood that there isn't any good work a man can do to earn salvation. Salvation can only be received as a free gift from God. Therefore. . .

- Because God loves us, He sent His Son into the world.
- Because God loves us, He offered up His Son for us that we

might be made righteous by the blood of the Lamb.

- Because God loves us, we receive the Holy Spirit when we turn to Christ in faith.

When Jesus saves us we enter into relationship with Him. We *know* Him and *He knows us*! We will never hear the words, "I never knew you: depart from me." But for those who are counting on their own good works to earn a place in the Kingdom of Heaven, although they may think they know Jesus, they will hear Him say, *"I never knew you: depart from me, ye that work iniquity."* (Matthew 7:23)

Remember there are wolves who look like sheep, thorns that look like grapes, thistles that look like figs, and there are also non-Christians who look like Christians, because of their words or their good works. Our words and our works are a reflection of what's in our hearts. If these people truly knew Jesus they would be praising His works, not their own. If these people truly knew Jesus, they would say...but for the grace You have given me I am not worthy of Your Kingdom.

Share the gospel of saving grace with someone today. Be faithful to proclaim the goodness of the Lord. **It's all about Jesus!** Help people to understand that only by trusting in Jesus' finished work will they have eternal life with Him and one day enter into the Kingdom of Heaven.

Jesus told us that He is preparing a place for those who trust in Him and He has promised, *"I will come again, and receive you unto myself; that where I am, there ye may be also."* (John 14: 3)

We receive that promise because we belong to Jesus.

"I am the way, the truth, and the life. No one comes to the Father except through Me." (John 14:6)

*Jesus

There is only one place in the world where evil, justice, love and forgiveness converged — on a hill called Calvary — *Ravi Zacharias*

Q. 2

What's the controversy about Mark 16:9-20?

Q. I was asked recently by a friend why the book of Mark has multiple endings in the last chapter, how can we tell which are reliable, and where should the chapter end? I couldn't give an answer that satisfied either myself or my friend. Can you help?

This is an interesting topic of great debate. There are a number of variations in the different translations for the ending of Mark chapter 16. They include:

1) Mark 16:9-20 is included

2) Mark 16:9-20 is omitted

3) Mark 16:9-20 is included with a statement after verse 8 and preceding verse 9 that reads: "But they reported briefly to Peter and those with him all that they had been told. And after this Jesus himself sent out by means of them, from east to west, the sacred and imperishable proclamation of eternal salvation"

4) Mark 16:9-20 is included with the verses placed in brackets to indicate it was not in the original, or with some type of disclaimer between verses 14 and 15. Some of the disclaimers include:

- Only found in one Greek manuscript-Codex Washingtonianus
- Some of the earliest manuscripts do not include 16:9-20
- Longer ending of Mark
- Mark 16:9 Later mss [manuscripts] add verses 9-20

Scholars have debated this issue for centuries. It's important to note that the variations are seen in relation to the differences in manuscript evidence.

Understanding Manuscript Evidence

There are two lines of Bible manuscripts. One originated in Antioch, Syria and is commonly referred to as the Antioch line. The other is referred to as the Alexandrian line, because it originated in Alexandria, Egypt. All modern translations derive from one of these two lines of manuscripts.

All translations from the Alexandrian line will have some form of exception to the Mark 16:9-20 passage (omission, insertion of additional information, or a disclaimer). The only Bibles that include Mark 16:9-20 with no exceptions are the King James Bible (KJV) and the New King James Version (NKJV), both of which come from the Antioch line of manuscripts.

When doing any research into the origins and trustworthiness of the Bible, always remember that God promised to preserve His Word:

> *Matthew 24:35 Heaven and earth shall pass away, but my words shall not pass away.*

The oldest manuscripts, the Vaticanus and Sinaiticus, are from the Alexandrian line of manuscripts. Those manuscripts do not include Mark 16:9-20, which explains why modern translations from the Alexandrian line will always include exceptions.

Remember, since Mark 16:9-20 is included in the manuscripts that originated in Antioch, the KJV and the NKJV do not have any exceptions.

Message of the text

Those who hold to the inclusion of Mark 16:9-20, without any exception, will claim that the omission of the passage leaves the book of Mark ending in fear. Without those last 12 verses, the book ends with Mark 16:8, which reads:

Mark 16:8 And they went out quickly, and fled from the sepulchre; for they trembled and were amazed: neither said they any thing to any man; for they were afraid.

If Mark 16:9-20 is omitted, there is no account of the resurrection recorded in the book of Mark. This would make it inconsistent with the other gospel accounts of Jesus' life, death, burial...*and* resurrection.

Questions to Consider

Is this an issue about the oldest record or God's Word being the most accurate? Or, is it more important that there be an extensive number of manuscripts to confirm the accuracy of the Word? There are more than 5,200 manuscripts in the Antioch line, but only 45 manuscripts in the Alexandrian. However, the Alexandrian line has the oldest manuscript. So which carries more authority? Older manuscripts or significantly more manuscripts?

Is this an issue of the completeness of the gospel account? Did the Vaticanus and Sinaiticus omit verses 9-20? Or, did the Antioch texts add those verses? Would the account in Mark most likely have been parallel to the other three gospels, which means it would have included the verses about the resurrection? Or, could there have been a reason why it was omitted?

I repeat, scholars have debated this issue for centuries. Therefore, I will not give a definitive answer, but I will share my opinion.

I believe that the Gospel of Mark would have included the entire passage of Mark 16:9-20. It seems more plausible that, rather than ending the account with the disciples in fear, Mark would close with the resurrection and with the disciples encouraged and empowered to serve the Lord—as revealed in verses 19 and 20.

Mark 16:19-20 So then after the Lord had spoken unto them, he was received up into heaven, and sat on the right hand of God. And they went forth, and preached every where, the Lord working with them, and confirming the word with signs following. Amen.

I also do not believe that older manuscripts hold more authority. Perhaps they are older and still remain because they were not well accepted, or they were not often read. The Bible that is read often will show signs of wear and might even fall apart from constant use. A Bible that is seldom used will remain intact and last for centuries. Perhaps the most reliable manuscripts were more frequently copied and read and therefore the Antioch manuscripts are not as old as the Alexandrian manuscripts.

The grass withers, And its flower falls away, but the word of the LORD endures forever. — Peter

(1 Peter 1:24-25)

There is much more to consider on this topic of debate. I encourage you to do further study and come to your own conclusions. Whatever you decide, regarding which manuscript line you prefer, remember that it is the Holy Spirit who teaches us. If God can speak through a donkey (and He did), then the Holy Spirit can certainly speak through any translation of God's Word.

Since no one can go back in time and evaluate the original documents, perhaps this is one of those cases in which we echo the words of the prophets Jeremiah (15:15) and Ezekiel (37:3) who said:

Oh Lord, thou knowest.

Q. 3

What is soul sleep?

Soul sleep is a false doctrine that teaches when a person dies, his soul "sleeps" and that it will not be made alive until the time of the bodily resurrection. During this time of "sleep" the person is not aware, or conscious, of their condition or state. It is falsely believed that the soul resides in the memory of God until it is made alive again. Seventh Day Adventists teach this.

Jehovah's Witnesses teach a variation of this doctrine. They believe in annihilation—a teaching that claims the body and soul cease to exist at death. Similar to the Seventh Day Adventists, Jehovah's Witnesses believe that the soul lies in this state of death until it is made alive in the bodily resurrection.

Both groups are in error about soul sleep. Although they use Scripture to support their beliefs, they do so incorrectly, such as with this verse from Ecclesiastes:

> *Ecclesiastes 9:5 For the living know that they shall die: but the dead know not any thing, neither have they any more a reward; for the memory of them is forgotten.*

This verse needs to be understood in context. These are "*The words of the Preacher, the son of David, king in Jerusalem*" (Ecclesiastes 1:1), and he is speaking from a human, or earthly, perspective about death. He is not making doctrinal statements about the condition of the soul after death. He is not saying that the soul dies, or enters into an unconscious state, at death. He is speaking of a person's earthly existence ceasing.

What does the Bible say about our soul after death?

In the New Testament we find clear teachings about the condition of the soul after death. Paul, with full knowledge and understanding of the redemption of sin by Christ's death on the cross and eternal life made possible by His resurrection, speaks of our physical death and the resurrection of the soul:

2 Corinthians 5:8 We are confident, I say, and willing rather to be absent from the body, and to be present with the Lord.

Paul is clearly saying that, when he dies, he will go and be with the Lord. He does not say, t*o be absent from the body, and to* [someday in the future] *be present with the Lord.* Paul also says,

For I am in a strait betwixt two, having a desire to depart, and to be with Christ; which is far better: (Philippians 1:23)

If Paul had thought his soul would be sleeping for a period of time, he would not have desired to die. Based upon his devotion to Christ and his commitment to spreading the gospel, he would have preferred to live and serve Christ. Paul says he has a *"desire to depart, and to be with Christ,"* right after he had just said, *"For to me to live is Christ, and to die is gain." (Philippians 1:21)*

When Paul said *"to live is Christ"* he was saying that his purpose and meaning in life came from knowing and serving Christ, especially in preaching the gospel. With that in mind, *"to die"* would not have been gain if his soul were to sleep. But Paul says it "*is gain*" (verse 21), because Paul knew that when he would die, he would go *"to be with Christ"* (verse 23) in Heaven.

Another precious teaching in this verse is that Paul knew that while he remained here on earth, Christ was here with him. He said, *"to live is Christ."* Christ is here with every believer, because the Holy Spirit, the third Person of the Trinity, indwells all believers.

The Death of the Body

At the time of our physical death the body returns to dust:

Ecclesiastes 12:7 Then shall the dust return to the earth as it was...

Genesis 3:19 In the sweat of thy face shalt thou eat bread, till thou return unto the ground; for out of it wast thou taken: for dust thou art, and unto dust shalt thou return.

Remember, Adam was created from the dust of the ground:

Genesis 2:7 And the LORD God formed man of the dust of the ground, and breathed into his nostrils the breath of life; and became a living soul.

You don't have a soul; you are a soul. You have a body...temporarily.
— original author unknown

So the body returns to where it came from, the ground. Ecclesiastes tells that the spirit returns to the Person who gave it, God.

Ecclesiastes 12:7 Then shall the dust return to the earth as it was: and the spirit shall return unto God who gave it.

This verse is speaking of the spirit of man that returns to God who gave it, for judgment. Whether it is an unregenerate spirit or a spirit made alive by the Holy Spirit, God will judge both at the time of death. Remember Hebrews 9:27 tells us, *And as it is appointed unto men once to die, but after this the judgment.*

Ecclesiastes 3:21 confirms this, *Who knoweth the spirit of man that goeth upward, and the spirit of the beast that goeth downward to the earth?*

The spirit of a beast (animal) goes into the ground, but man's spirit goes to God. Remember that man is an eternal being. All souls will live eternally after the bodily death. The question is not *whether* man will spend eternity somewhere, but rather *where* man will spend eternity.

Jesus' Teaching Denies Soul Sleep

Jesus' account of Lazarus and the rich man in Luke 16 clearly shows that soul sleep is a false teaching. Both men are bodily dead, but both men are fully aware of their condition and their location.

Luke 16:22-28 And it came to pass, that the beggar died, and was carried by the angels into Abraham's bosom: the rich man also died, and was buried; And in hell he lift up his eyes, being in torments, and seeth Abraham afar off, and Lazarus in his bosom. . . between us and you there is a great gulf fixed: so that they which would pass from hence to you cannot; neither can they pass to us, that would come from thence. Then he said, I pray thee therefore, father, that thou wouldest send him to my father's house: For I have five brethren; that he may testify unto them, lest they also come into this place of torment.

Both of these men had experienced physical death and yet the souls of both lived on. There are many more verses that support our souls going to be with the Lord at the time of our physical death. We know that the body dies, so Jesus' words in these verses are regarding the soul:

John 11:25-26 Jesus said unto her, I am the resurrection, and the life: he that believeth in me, though he were dead, yet shall he live: And whosoever liveth and believeth in me shall never die.

And it's clear in these verse that these souls are not sleeping:

Revelation 6:9-10 And when he had opened the fifth seal, I saw under the altar the souls of them that were slain for the word of God, and for the testimony which they held: And they cried with a loud voice, saying, How long, O Lord, holy and true, dost thou not judge and avenge our blood on them that dwell on the earth?

And perhaps one of the best verses is Luke 23:43, *And Jesus said unto him, Verily I say unto thee, To day shalt thou be with me in paradise.*

Praise the Lord that when we die
we immediately go to be with Him!!!

Q. 4

Are you certain that when we die we go to be with the Lord?

A member of the Reasons for Hope*Jesus community (identified here as CH) responded with a desire to further dialogue about soul sleep. CH's questions and comments are italicized. My response is designated SA.

CH: *Hello all the way from sunny South Africa! Thank you for this teaching on soul sleep. Before I begin, I'd like to say that I am a born again, God-fearing Christian and I love to read and study God's Word. Therefore I talk and debate about issues like this with an open and willing heart.*

I always thought that our spirits do "soul sleep" while our flesh is dead until the day of judgment, because of the following:

> *1 Corinthians 15:51 Behold, I shew you a mystery; We shall not all sleep, but we shall all be changed...*

In context, this verse is talking about the time when our Lord Jesus Christ returns—some call it the Rapture. What stands out in this verse is, "we shall not all sleep." That is talking about the dead.

+++

SA: Because Paul is talking about the time when Christ will come for His bride (the Rapture of the Church), Paul is saying that not all will die a *physical or bodily* death.

> *1 Corinthians 15:51 Behold, I show you a mystery; We* [who belong to Christ] *shall not all sleep* [bodily death], *but we shall all be changed.*

*Jesus

When Christ comes there will be those who belong to Christ, and are still living on earth—they too will "be changed." Paul goes on to confirm this by saying:

> *1 Corinthians 15:52 In a moment, in the twinkling of an eye, at the last trump: for the trumpet shall sound, and the* [bodily] *dead shall be raised incorruptible, and we* [all believers] *shall be changed [all believers will be changed, receiving glorified bodies, both those whose bodies lie dead in the grave and those who are alive at His coming for His Church].*

+++

CH: *In this verse we can also see that the dead are referred to as being asleep. And we can't say the verse is talking about the flesh because we know that the flesh can't inherit the kingdom of God!*

> *1 Thessalonians 4:15 "For this we say unto you by the word of the Lord, that we which are alive and remain unto the coming of the Lord shall not prevent them which are asleep."*

+++

SA: You are correct that flesh and blood will not inherit the Kingdom of God (1 Corinthians 15:50). Let's look at the verse you mention in a broader context:

> *1 Thessalonians 4:13-14 But I would not have you to be ignorant, brethren, concerning them which are asleep* [dead in the grave], *that ye sorrow not, even as others which have no hope. For if we believe that Jesus died and rose again, even so them also which sleep in Jesus* [the body is dead] *will God bring with him.*

Paul is speaking of the death of the body. In Scripture the word "sleep" is used often to mean physical, bodily death. For example, the witnesses to Christ's resurrection of whom Paul says:

> *1 Corinthians 15:6 After that, he was seen of above five hundred brethren at once; of whom the greater part remain unto this pres-*

> *ent, but some are fallen asleep.* [They have died a physical death. Paul is saying they no longer live to testify.]

Scripture tells us that the *"wages of sin is death"* (Romans 6:23)—that death is both a spiritual and a physical death for all people. However, Jesus conquered physical death, and, just as we are made alive when we are born again, one day our bodies will be miraculously resurrected. Believers' bodies will be raised to glorification and non-believers to condemnation.

Let's look at a question Paul raises in 1 Corinthians, and then two errors that he addresses regarding the bodily resurrection.

> *1 Corinthians 15:35 But some man will say, How are the dead raised up? and with what body do they come?*

Error #1) Some believe the *same* body in the grave will rise. Paul explains it will be a different body—a body given by God:

> *1 Corinthians 15:38 But God giveth it a body as it hath pleased him, and to every seed his own body.*

Error #2) The risen body is *unrelated* to the body that previously lay dead in the grave. It is the body, made-alive, yet different:

> *1 Corinthians 15:36 Thou fool, that which thou sowest is not quickened, except it die.*

> *1 Corinthians 15:39-41 All flesh is not the same flesh: but there is one kind of flesh of men, another flesh of beasts, another of fishes, and another of birds. There are also celestial bodies, and bodies terrestrial: but the glory of the celestial is one, and the glory of the terrestrial is another. There is one glory of the sun, and another glory of the moon, and another glory of the stars: for one star differeth from another star in glory.*

The Bible tells us that we will receive glorified bodies:

> *Philippians 3:20-21 For our conversation* [citizenship] *is in*

> *heaven; from whence also we look for the Saviour, the Lord Jesus Christ: Who shall change our vile body* [the human body, changed at the rapture], *that it may be fashioned like unto his glorious body* [the promise of a glorified body], *according to the working whereby he is able even to subdue all things unto himself.*

Only the Lord can "awaken," make alive, believers' dead bodies. When Jesus comes for His bride, those who are alive in physical bodies will also be made-alive with a new, glorified body.

+++

1 Thessalonians 4:16 "For the Lord himself shall descend from heaven with a shout, with the voice of the archangel, and with the trump of God: and the dead in Christ shall rise first:"

CH: *Why rise when you have already risen?*

+++

SA: Again, in context, this is about the bodily resurrection. It teaches that believers whose bodies lie in the grave will be made alive first. That includes, all believers who died in faith…both the Old Testament saints and New Covenant believers. Consider the verse referenced in a larger context:

> *1 Thessalonians 4:15-17 For this we say unto you by the word of the Lord, that we which are alive and remain unto the coming of the Lord* [those still living at this time] *shall not prevent them which are asleep.* [those who have died will be bodily raised first] *For the Lord himself shall descend from heaven with a shout, with the voice of the archangel, and with the trump of God: and the dead in Christ shall rise first: Then we which are alive and remain shall be caught up together with them in the clouds, to meet the Lord in the air: and so shall we ever be with the Lord.*

Our souls have risen to glory. They are already with the Lord, but in the bodily resurrection the "incorruptible" body will put on "immortality"—a new, glorified body (1 Corinthians 15:52-53)—and death will be swallowed up in victory.

1 Corinthians 15:54-55 So when this corruptible shall have put on incorruption, and this mortal shall have put on immortality, then shall be brought to pass the saying that is written, Death is swallowed up in victory. O death, where is thy sting? O grave, where is thy victory?

Remember again that Paul considered death to be "gain" (Philippians 1:21). If death brought an unconscious state, it would not be gain. Paul served the Lord with joyfulness on earth and he would have preferred to live and serve, than to lie in unconsciousness in the grave until the time of the Lord's return.

Paul clearly tells in 2 Corinthians 5:8 why he considered death to be gain: *We are confident, I say, and willing rather to be absent from the body, and to be present with the Lord.*

Paul is stating that the soul departs the body and goes to be forever in the Lord's presence. Revelation 6:9 tells of the souls under the altar who are conscious and in His presence. The account of Lazarus and the rich man in Luke 16 clear tells of both men being conscious. And of course we remember Jesus' words to the thief on the cross. Jesus told the thief that he would be with Him in Paradise that day. Jesus was not unconscious in Paradise. His body lay dead in the grave, but His soul was alive and He preached in Paradise. So the soul is clearly eternal and does not die or sleep.

+++

CH: *For me this is a "time" issue. God created time, therefore He exists outside its constraints, unlike us (2 Peter 3:8). Reading through the book of Revelation showed me not to think of the events in an ordered sequence. And for that reason I think our souls will be fully alive with God and dormant (sleeping) at the same time until the day of judgment.*

+++

SA: We agree that God created time and that He is outside of time. But that does not mean that our souls are both "fully alive" and "dormant" at the same time. Our souls are eternal, not temporal. As believers, our judgment took place at the cross. Our sins were paid for by Jesus and our souls were made alive at the time we repented and trusted in His finished work. "Made alive" means that we are given *eternal* life with Jesus. If our souls need to be "made alive" again, as soul sleep doctrines claim, then Christ did not conquer death. If our souls must be made alive again, then our salvation did not secure an eternal life with Him.

We know that while we live here on earth Christ is with us by the presence and power of His Holy Spirit indwelling us. When we die, we go immediately to be with Him. So we are, from the time of our salvation, eternally with Him.

Remember Jesus said He would never leave or forsake us (Hebrews 13:5). If our souls sleep in an unconscious state and the Holy Spirit is no longer with us, then we cease to have communion/relationship with Him. He said He would ***never*** leave us, so the concept of His being forever with us outside of our time dimension, *but not within our time dimension*, denies what Jesus said. There is no biblical support for the soul being both inside and outside of our time dimension. God is omnipresent, but we are not. Our souls could not be in both places at the same time.

Jesus prayed that we be united to Him as He and the Father are united (John 17:21). The Triune Godhead is co-eternal, for all eternity. We have that same assurance of unity in Him.

So with all this said, we stand firm on our belief that the souls of all people live eternally. They do not die, nor do they sleep. For believers, at the time of death, their souls go to be with the Lord. For non-believers their souls depart into the place of torment (Luke 16), awaiting a final judgment.

We encourage you to seek the Lord in prayer and to continue reading and studying His Word.

Whosoever believeth in him should not perish,
but have everlasting life. John 3:16

Q. 5

Do we live by Law or by grace?

Q. Do we still live by the Mosaic Law? Did the Law end with the death of Jesus? Do we live by Law or by grace? I have to answer this question for some people, but I am not sure myself. What does the Bible say about it?

In order to answer this, let's start by defining both the Mosaic Law and the grace of God. In doing so, we'll be able to determine what roles God's Law and His grace play in our lives.

What is Law?

The Law commonly refers to The 10 Commandments given to Moses on Mt. Sinai. The Ten Commandments are a reflection of the perfection of God and the perfect life that He calls us to (although we can never fully attain it).

Paul tells us that the "law is holy, and the commandments holy, and just, and good" (Romans 7:12). The Law is all those things, but also understand that the Law is not capable of saving anyone. Only Jesus can save sinners. When Jesus came and lived on earth, He kept the Law perfectly, which means that He honored God by living in accordance with God's will and did not break any of His commandments. That is something we cannot do.

> *Legalism says God will love us if we change. The gospel says God will change us because He loves us.*
>
> *— Tullian Tchividjian*

We are also reminded that Jesus did not abolish, destroy or do away with the Law. We are told that He fulfilled the Law.

Matthew 5:17 Do not think that I came to destroy the Law or the Prophets. I did not come to destroy but to fulfill.

What is grace?

Grace is being given something that we do not deserve—something that we have not earned. The gift of salvation is *"by grace... through faith"* in Jesus Christ (Ephesians 2:8). His death paid the penalty for our sins and His resurrection gives us life. The Lord's life, death, burial and resurrection is the good news—the gospel of saving grace. We cannot do anything to earn it. We can only receive it as a free gift of God, received through Christ who earned it for us.

Life by Law prevents love. Life by grace produces love.
-- Tullian Tchividjian

In addition to saving grace, there is also a sanctifying grace in the gospel of Jesus Christ. When we come to Christ in repentance and faith, and trust on His finished work on the cross, He saves us from the penalty of our sins. When He does this, He also gives us eternal life and the Person and presence of the Holy Spirit, who guides and teaches us in all things and convicts us of sin. That moment begins our life-long journey of sanctification on this earth. Sanctification is a process of growing in holiness and becoming more and more conformed to the image of our Saviour.

Romans 8:29 For whom he did foreknow, he also did predestinate to be conformed to the image of his Son, that he might be the firstborn among many brethren.

So the gospel not only saves us from the penalty of sin, it also gives us sanctifying grace that saves us from the power of sin by enabling us to overcome sin. We are not capable of conquering sin by our power, so God graciously gave us His Spirit:

Zechariah 4:6 Not by [your] *might, nor by* [your] *power, but* ***by my spirit****, saith the LORD of hosts.*

What purpose does the Law serve today?

Since the Law cannot save anyone, why is it good? The answer is that the Law is good because it reveals our sin to us.

Romans 3:20 ...for by the law is the knowledge of sin.

The Law is God's perfect standard for righteous living. We are to measure our behavior by God's standard. It is only when we see and understand our sin that we can repent and turn from our sin and turn to Christ. The Law works in the lives of all people.

1) The Law works in the lives of the lost to reveal their sin and to bring them to saving faith (salvation in Christ).

2) The Law works in the lives of believers to reveal their sin and to grow them in sanctifying faith (growing in holiness).

The Grace of God

In His last words on the cross Jesus said, "It is finished." As Christians, we know that His finished work on the cross paid the penalty for our sins and opened the way to eternal life. That same grace that saved us from our sins in our justification is also active in saving us in our everyday walk in faith (sanctification). "It is finished" is true in our justification, and, in our sanctification, it is the Lord's finished work and His gift of the Holy Spirit that grows us in holiness and conforms us to His image (Romans 8:29).

The Law-maker (God) became the Law-keeper (Jesus) and died for us, the Law-breakers.

— Tullian Tchividjian

Preach the gospel to yourself every day, remembering Jesus' life, death, burial and resurrection. Remember that He has forgiven every sin you have ever committed, or ever will commit.

Colossians 2:13-14 And you, being dead in your trespasses and the uncircumcision of your flesh, He has made alive together with Him, having forgiven you all trespasses, having wiped out the handwriting of requirements that was against us, which was contrary to us. And He has taken it out of the way, having nailed it to the cross.

Run, John, run, the law commands
But gives us neither feet nor hands,
Far better news the gospel brings:
It bids us fly and gives us wings.
— John Bunyon

Remember also the power of the Holy Spirit who equips and empowers you to grow in your love and knowledge of Jesus Christ.

The answer to the question, "Do we live by Law or grace," is:

We live IN His grace and BY His grace.

As Christians, who have repented and trusted in Christ's finished work, we live *in* the grace of His gift of salvation and we live *by* the grace of His Spirit indwelling us. Remembering His grace will equip, encourage and empower us to understand and love His Law as another gift of grace…the "picture" of the holiness and glory of God—the holiness that we will one day attain and the glory that we will one day behold.

1 Corinthians 13:12 For now we see through a glass, darkly; but then face to face: now I know in part; but then shall I know even as also I am known.

Remember this: the ***Law will* reveal** the sin in your life, but only ***grace will* restore** you to God and only by grace can you ***rest in Christ.***

We live by Grace!!!

Q. 6

Why do I feel unforgiven?

Q. I keep asking God to forgive me for something I did that was very bad, but I don't feel like He has forgiven me. Why do I feel this way?

The fact that you asked God to forgive you shows that the Holy Spirit is active in your life and He is convicting you of sin. 1 John 1:9 reminds us that,

If we confess our sins, he is faithful and just to forgive us our sins, and to cleanse us from all unrighteousness.

Because you have *already* confessed your sin, you are *already* forgiven and cleansed. Remember, when Christ said, "*It is finished*" (John 19:30), He pronounced that the penalty for sin was paid in full. Your sins, past, present and future have all been nailed to His cross (Colossians 2:14) and His blood has paid the price for your redemption (Ephesians 1:7).

Forgiveness is the key that unlocks the door of resentment and the handcuffs of hatred. It is a power that breaks the chains of bitterness and the shackles of selfishness.
— Corrie ten Boom

Remember, your sins were forgiven the moment you repented and trusted in Christ. You already have His forgiveness. It is finished. You are sealed, forever!

Now also remember, God *does* want us to continue in confessing and repenting of sin. In doing so it draws us closer to Him. The cleansing we receive is one of living more fully in the gospel — the good news that Christ loves us and has secured for us the forgiveness of our sins.

So, why do you still feel unforgiven? Two possible reasons:

1) You are still dwelling on the grievous nature of your sin.

2) You have not repented of your sin.

Dwelling on Sin

God has forgiven you, but perhaps you are having trouble forgiving yourself. You honor God when you believe and receive His forgiveness. Remember His promises that, in Christ, He has…

What though the vile accuser roar
Of sins that I have done;
I know them well,
and thousands more
My God, He knoweth none

My sin is cast into the sea
Of God's forgotten memory
No more to haunt accusingly
For Christ has lived and died
for me

-- His be the Victor's Name
Words by Samuel Gandy, 1838;
alt. lyrics by Zac Hicks 2013

Forgiven You

Psalm 103:12 As far as the east is from the west, so far hath he removed our transgressions from us.

Cleansed You

Revelation 1:5 And from Jesus Christ, who is the faithful witness, and the first begotten of the dead, and the prince of the kings of the earth. Unto him that loved us, and washed us from our sins in his own blood,

Forgotten Your Sin

Hebrews 8:12 For I will be merciful to their unrighteousness, and their sins and their iniquities will I remember no more.

The devil may desire that you dwell on past sins, but remember you have victory in the cross of Jesus Christ.

1 John 5:4 For whatsoever is born of God overcometh the world: and this is the victory that overcometh the world, even our faith.

Honor the Lord by believing and trusting that He has forgiven You. He has promised that you are forgiven, and He is faithful to keep His Word.

Failure to Repent

Repentance means "to turn." If you continue to commit the same sin, ask the Lord to strengthen you to repent—to turn from the sin and to gain victory over it through Jesus Christ. He has promised you the power to do so. When He saved you, He gave you the power and presence of His Holy Spirit.

To do so no more is the truest repentance.
— Martin Luther

1 John 4:4 ..greater is he that is in you, than he that is in the world.

Remember, the Holy Spirit is not only greater than our adversary the devil, He is also greater than our flesh, our worldly desires and our human weakness. And therefore…

Romans 8:37. . .we are more than conquerors through him that loved us.

Remember also that feelings can lie and deceive us. Confess and repent of sin and with faith and trust in the Lord receive the forgiveness He has already given you. BELIEVE that you are cleansed. Rejoice in the gospel. Rejoice in the forgiveness you already have…

Philippians 4:4 Rejoice in the Lord always: and again I say, Rejoice.

Finally, believe that God will help you to grow in righteousness.

Now unto him that is able to keep you from falling, and to present you faultless before the presence of his glory with exceeding joy, To the only wise God our Saviour, be glory and majesty, dominion and power, both now and for ever. Amen. (Jude 1:24-25)

There is only one place in the world where evil,
justice, love and forgiveness converged —
on a hill called Calvary — Ravi Zacharias

Q. 7

Who Killed Jesus?

This is a question that we all must answer. Let's begin by looking at what the Bible says about what took place regarding the betrayal, the arrest, the trial and the crucifixion of Jesus.

Jesus was betrayed by Judas, one of His followers.

Luke 22:47-48 And while he yet spake, behold a multitude, and he that was called Judas, one of the twelve, went before them, and drew near unto Jesus to kiss him. But Jesus said unto him, Judas, betrayest thou the Son of man with a kiss?

The Jews denied Jesus and Peter said they killed Him.
On the day of Pentecost, after healing a lame man, Peter said...

Acts 3:12-15 ...Ye men of Israel, why marvel ye at this? or why look ye so earnestly on us, as though by our own power or holiness we had made this man to walk? The God of Abraham, and of Isaac, and of Jacob, the God of our fathers, hath glorified his Son Jesus; whom ye delivered up, and denied him in the presence of Pilate, when he was determined to let him go. But ***ye denied the Holy One*** *and the Just, and desired a murderer to be granted unto you;* ***And killed the Prince of life****, whom God hath raised from the dead; whereof we are witnesses.*

Roman soldiers arrested Jesus.

The group of men who came to arrest Jesus was composed of Roman soldiers, Jewish servants, and Judas:

John 18:12-13 Then the band and the captain and officers of the Jews took Jesus, and bound him, And led him away to Annas first...

Jesus was tried in a Jewish court.

Although this court had no authority to execute a death penalty, Jesus stood before Caiphas in a Jewish court for judgment.

John 18:14 Now Caiaphas was he, which gave counsel to the Jews, that it was expedient that one man should die for the people.

Jesus was handed over to a Roman court.

When Jesus stood before Pontius Pilate in the Roman court, Pilate called together the chief priests, rulers and the people and said unto them:

Luke 23:13-16 Ye have brought this man unto me, as one that perverteth the people: and, behold, I, having examined him before you, have found no fault in this man touching those things whereof ye accuse him: No, nor yet Herod: for I sent you to him; and, lo, nothing worthy of death is done unto him. I will therefore chastise him, and release him.

We are more wicked than we ever dared believe, but more loved and accepted in Christ than we ever dared hope.
— Tim Keller

Because it was "of necessity" (Luke 23:17) to release a prisoner during the time of the Feast of Passover, Pilate offered to release Jesus, but in response the Jews chose the release of another:

Luke 23:18 ...they cried out all at once, saying, Away with this man, and release unto us Barabbas.

The Question Remains
The Answer is Clear

Since the first century AD, a debate has existed regarding who killed Jesus. Was it Judas? The Jews? The Romans? The answer is really quite simple.

I killed Jesus. You killed Jesus. Since the day that Adam ate the forbidden fruit in the Garden, everyone who has ever lived, or ever will live, killed Jesus. It is our sin that demands atonement, and only Jesus could make the payment for our sins. It was your sins, my sins, everyone's sins, that cried out "crucify Him," and so Jesus offered Himself, a willing sacrifice, to pay for our sins and satisfy a just and righteous God .

Rembrandt's famous painting, *Raising of the Cross*, clearly portrays an understanding of the personal responsibility each one of us must accept and confess.

Rembrandt, *Raising of the Cross* (c. 1633) Alte Pinakothek, Munich

Rembrandt painted this amazing portrait of Christ nailed to the cross and being lifted up. Noteworthy in this masterpiece is that Rembrandt inserted himself into the painting—an indication that he understood he also was responsible for the death of the Son of Man. Just as Rembrandt understood his guilt, we all must understand that we are guilty. It is our sin that put Jesus on the cross, and it is our sin for which He died.

For those of us who understand our sin and have come to the foot of the cross in repentance, faith and trust, Jesus' blood has washed us clean. Adam's sin brought our condemnation, but Christ's righteousness paid our ransom and cleansed us.

As you look at this painting, imagine yourself standing there. See your sin that cost so much. See your Saviour who gave so much. See Him lifted up, and remember He did this willingly for you. Then remember He conquered death and rose again, opening the way to Heaven and eternal life in Him.

Hallelujah what a Saviour!

Romans 3:10 There is none righteous, no, not one.

We are all sinners fallen short of the glory of God. Without the blood of Jesus, all are unrighteous in His eyes. But God promised...

Isaiah 1:18 ...though your sins be as scarlet, they shall be as white as snow; though they be red like crimson, they shall be as wool.

Not only at Easter, but all year through, commit to remembering every day...

Jesus Christ, who is the faithful witness, and the first begotten of the dead, and the prince of the kings of the earth. Unto him that loved us, and washed us from our sins in his own blood, And hath made us kings and priests unto God and his Father; to him be glory and dominion for ever and ever. Amen. (Revelation 1:5-6)

Q. 8

Why didn't the Jews accept Jesus as the Messiah?

The simple answer is that the Jews were looking for a King who would free them from Roman oppression. They were not looking for a Suffering Servant who would die for them. The Jews wanted the Lion of the Tribe of Judah, not the Lamb of God.

Throughout the Old Testament God prepared His chosen people to wait for their coming Messiah and to be ready to recognize Him at His coming. The promise was made in the Garden of Eden, right after the fall of man:

> *Genesis 3:15 And I will put enmity between thee and the woman, and between thy seed and her seed; it shall bruise thy head, and thou shalt bruise his heel.*

God promised that the seed of the women (Jesus) would come and bruise the head of the serpent (Satan). Jesus did just that, but not in the way the Jews expected. Therefore when Jesus came, the Jews did not recognize their Messiah.

The Passover

Consider the spring feast of Passover, an annual feast that dated back to Israel's deliverance out of Egypt and from Egyptian bondage. Every part of the feast pointed to a coming Saviour and Messiah, and in Jesus' first coming He fulfilled this feast and the promise God made in the Garden.

Jesus lived a perfect, sinless life, and on the 10th day of the month of Nisan, the day in which the Passover lamb was selected, Jesus presented Himself as the Lamb of God and rode into Jerusalem on a donkey (Matthew 21:5-9).

During the next four days, He was challenged and tested by the Pharisees and the rulers, just as the Passover lambs were kept in the homes and inspected for four days to determine whether they were pure and without spot (Exodus 12:5-6). Jesus passed every test and on the 14th of Nisan, at the same time the Passover lambs were being slain, Jesus *our Passover Lamb* was crucified. As the blood of the Passover lambs was drained out, our Passover Lamb's blood was poured out—for our sins.

Either sin is with you, lying on your shoulders, or it is lying on Christ, the Lamb of God. Now if it is lying on your back, you are lost; but if it is resting on Christ, you are free, and you will be saved. Now choose what you want.

— Martin Luther

Just as the blood of the first Passover lambs (Exodus 12) was placed over the doors of the Israelites' homes to protect them from the angel of death during the final plague in Egypt, Jesus' blood covers us (Romans 4:7). Not only does it cover us, His blood also removes our sin (Psalm 103:12). We are washed by His blood (Revelation 1:5) and "made free from the law of sin and death" (Romans 8:2).

The Jews did not understand that the Passover was fulfilled in the Jesus Christ. They were looking for a coming King, to free them from Roman oppression. On the 10th of Nisan, the day we call Palm Sunday, the Jews hailed Jesus as King (John 12:13), but a short 4 days later, they demanded "crucify Him" (John 19:6, 15). He was not what they had hoped for or expected.

To this day the Jews do not recognize the Suffering Servant, who died on the cross. They claim Jesus did not fulfill these prophecies:

Building the third Temple (Ezekiel 37:26-28)

Regathering of all Jews back to Israel (Isaiah 43:5-6)

Ushering in world peace, freedom from hate, oppression, suffering and disease (Isaiah 2:4)
Spreading universal knowledge of the God of Israel and uniting humanity as one (Zechariah 14:9).

The Jews are correct that Jesus did not do those things in His first advent. In His humble incarnation, Jesus came to live a perfect, sinless life—the life we cannot live—and then to die the death that we should die. He died for our sins, paying the penalty for them and absorbing the wrath of God that should have been poured out upon us. In doing so He made available forgiveness of sins to all who come to Him in repentance and trust in His finished work on the cross. One day Jesus will come again, and He will fulfill all of the remaining prophecies.

He will come as the King of Kings and Lord of Lords:

Revelation 19:11 And I saw heaven opened, and behold a white horse; and he that sat upon him was called Faithful and True, and in righteousness he doth judge and make war.

Revelation 19:16 And he hath on his vesture and on his thigh a name written, KING OF KINGS, AND LORD OF LORDS.

He will judge the living and the dead:

2 Timothy 4:1 I charge you therefore before God and the Lord Jesus Christ, who will judge the living and the dead at His appearing and His kingdom:

He will make ALL things new:

Revelation 21:5 And he that sat upon the throne said, Behold, I make all things new. And he said unto me, Write: for these words are true and faithful.

The Lamb Before the King

A most significant point that the Jews and other non-believers do not realize is that without the blood of the Passover Lamb, you don't want the coming King. The King will come in judgment and He will judge the world.

> *Acts 17:30-31 "Truly, these times of ignorance God overlooked, but now commands all men everywhere to repent, because He has appointed a day on which He will judge the world in righteousness by the Man whom He has ordained. He has given assurance of this to all by raising Him from the dead."*

If you don't have the forgiveness of sins, that only the Lamb of God can give you (John 1:29), then on judgment day you will be condemned. For those who trust in Jesus Christ and have received His forgiveness, we are promised:

> *Romans 8:1-2 There is therefore now no condemnation to those who are in Christ Jesus, who do not walk according to the flesh, but according to the Spirit. For the law of the Spirit of life in Christ Jesus has made me free from the law of sin and death.*

Because Jesus died the death we should have died and paid the penalty for our sins, we are forgiven. Because Jesus rose again conquering death, we have eternal life in Him.

Commit to sharing the gospel of saving grace everyday. Everywhere we go, there are dead people walking. Tell them how they can have life and have it to the fullest. Jesus proclaimed...

...I am come that they might have life,
and that they might have it more abundantly.
John 10:10

Q. 9

Where did Jesus go when He died?

The Bible is really quite clear on this. Jesus' soul went to Abraham's Bosom and his body went into the grave. Remember Jesus referred to being in the *"heart of the earth"* for *"three days and three nights."*

> *Matthew 12:40 For as Jonas was three days and three nights in the whale's belly; so shall the Son of man be three days and three nights in the heart of the earth.*

The "heart of the earth" is also referred to as Abraham's Bosom (Luke 16). Prior to Jesus' resurrection, at death a person's soul either went to Abraham's Bosom or to the place of torment.

> *Luke 16:22-23 And it came to pass, that the beggar died, and was carried by the angels into Abraham's bosom: the rich man also died, and was buried; And in hell he lift up his eyes, being in torments, and seeth Abraham afar off, and Lazarus in his bosom.*

In verse 23 "hell" is the Greek word "hades," defined as the place of departed souls. Today we use the word hell to exclusively mean the place of torment, but prior to the cross the place of the departed souls (hell/hades) had two chambers. One was a place of comfort, Abraham's bosom—the resting place of the Old Testament saints. The other was the place of torment, which today we refer to as hell.

Jesus clearly said He would be in *"the heart of the earth"* (Matthew 12:40, above). 1 Peter also tells us that during the three days Jesus was in the "heart of the earth" he preached to the spirits in prison (the place of torment).

1 Peter 3:18-19 For Christ also hath once suffered for sins, the just for the unjust, that he might bring us to God, being put to death in the flesh, but quickened by the Spirit: By which also he went and preached unto the spirits in prison.

There is a center to the Bible and its message of grace. It is Jesus Christ. Grace must therefore be preached in a way that is centered and focused on Jesus, never offering the benefits of the gospel without the Benefactor Himself.
— Sinclair Ferguson

Prior to the cross, both Abraham's Bosom and the place of torment existed in the earth. In Ephesians we are told that when Jesus "ascended up on high," He led the Old Testament saints to Heaven.

Ephesians 4:8-10 Wherefore he saith, When he ascended up on high, he led captivity captive, and gave gifts unto men. (Now that he ascended, what is it but that he also descended first into the lower parts of the earth? He that descended is the same also that ascended up far above all heavens, that he might fill all things.)

In doing so, Jesus fulfilled the prophecy of Psalm 68:18

Thou hast ascended on high, thou hast led captivity captive: thou hast received gifts for men...

Remember at the time of Jesus' death His soul went to the place of comfort, Abraham's Bosom, and He remained there three days and three nights, just as He said He would (Matthew 12:40). He then rose; and, when He ascended into Heaven, He took with Him the souls of Old Testament saints (fulfilling Psalm 68:18). Now the only abode of the dead in the earth is the place of torment—hell.

O death, where is thy sting? O grave, where is thy victory? The sting of death is sin; and the strength of sin is the law. But thanks be to God, which giveth us the victory through our Lord Jesus Christ. 1 Corinthians 15:55-57

Q. 10

How could God allow people to suffer in hell?

In answering this question (and all questions), we need to start with remembering who God is and what He has done for us.

Who God Is

Remember that God is both loving and just. He created the earth, and all that is in it, to be in perfect harmony with Him and His purpose and plan.

> *Genesis 1:31 And God saw every thing that he had made, and, behold, it was very good.*

When Adam disobeyed God, both sin and corruption entered into the world. But God, in His great love for His creation, promised a deliverer (Genesis 3:15) and in time He sent Jesus to redeem the world. He paid the penalty for our sin and will one day make all things new.

What God Has Done for Us

God sent Jesus, who lived as a man and died in our place, securing forgiveness of sins. He offer the gift of salvation to all who repent and trust in Him.

> *Ephesians 1:7 In Whom we have redemption through his blood, the forgiveness of sins, according to the riches of his grace...*

When a sinner trusts in Christ's finished work on the cross to pay for their sins, their sins are forgiven and Christ's righteousness is imputed (credited) to them. The forgiven sinner is then righteous because of his standing in Christ.

*Jesus

> *There are two kinds of people: those who say to God, 'Thy will be done,' and those to whom God says, 'All right, then, have it your way.'*
> — *C. S. Lewis*

Romans 4:24 But for us also, to whom it [righteousness] *shall be imputed, if we believe on him that raised up Jesus our Lord from the dead...*

Understanding God's plan of redemption, and remembering His loving kindness, let's return to the question: How could a loving God allow people to suffer for eternity in hell?

God Will Judge All Sin

Jesus took upon Himself our sin and paid for it with His blood. For the person who has repented and trusted in Christ, his sin was judged on the cross (Ephesians 1:7) and they have received forgiveness.

God will also judge the sin of those who die in unrepentant/unforgiven sin—those who have not been washed in Christ's blood (Revelation 1:5) and are without the covering of Christ's imputed righteousness. Those people will be judged by their works, and they will be found guilty. The Bible tells us that "*the wages of sin is death*" (Romans 6:23) and that there is a place prepared for the unrighteous. We know it as hell, and sadly it is a place of torment.

God is Loving, Kind and Just

Jesus told that God's Law requires perfection when He said, "*Be ye therefore perfect, even as your Father which is in heaven is perfect.*" (Matthew 5:48) Everything God created was perfect and God requires perfection. Since we can't achieve it, God, in His kindness and love, provided the only way for fallen man to obtain it.

Let us remember that the only reason someone will suffer for eternity in hell is because they have rejected the provision God gave for the forgiveness of their sins and therefore have not received the imputed righteousness of Jesus Christ.

John 3:18-19 He that believeth on him is not condemned: but ***he***

> ***that believeth not is condemned already**, because he hath not believed in the name of the only begotten Son of God. And this is the condemnation, that light is come into the world, and men loved darkness rather than light, because their deeds were evil.*

God does not desire that anyone should perish, but that all would come to Christ (2 Peter 3:9)—that all would come to the Light. Jesus spoke of Himself in John 3:18-19 as the light that is *"come into the world."* He also spoke of the choice each person makes. One choice is to choose light by repenting and trusting in Christ. The other is choosing darkness by a rejection of Christ and His offer of salvation. Those who choose light receive eternal life. Those who reject the Light are "condemned already" by their choice. Sadly, they will die in their sins and live eternally in hell.

In our love for others, it is very difficult to think about our friends and family perishing. But remember, they perish because of their choice to reject God's gift of mercy and grace. Their works will never be good enough and they will stand before God unrighteousness in His eyes.

When it breaks our hearts to think that someone we love might die in their sins, we should consider how we might share God's love and grace with them. Let the just judgment of our righteous God be a motivation to share the gospel of saving grace with a lost and dying world. We don't want anyone to die in their sins and face an eternity in hell. Christ died that all might come to know Him and be found righteous in the eyes of God.

Remember the blessings of forgiveness of your sins and the imputed righteousness that you have received from God. Share His love and saving grace with someone today.

...there is no God else beside me; a just God and a Saviour; there is none beside me. Look unto me, and be ye saved, all the ends of the earth: for I am God, and there is none else.

(Isaiah 45:21-22)

Behold, the former things are come to pass, and new things do I declare: before they spring forth I tell you of them. — *Isaiah 42:9*

Q. 11

Were we spirits before we were born?

The answer is no. The soul of man will live eternally (either in Heaven or in hell), but the soul of man did not exist in a spirit form (or any other form) prior to birth. The confusion about spiritual preexistence comes from Jeremiah 1:5.

> *Before I formed you in the womb I knew you; Before you were born I sanctified you; I ordained you a prophet to the nations.*

Since the Bible does not support any idea of the preexistence of man in any form, let's try to understand what this verse means.

"Before I formed you in the womb I knew you."

That raises the question, how did God know us before He formed us in the womb? There are two possible answers:

1) We existed in some form, and at some place, before we were formed in the womb (we've already stated that is not a biblical viewpoint).

2) God's omniscience (all knowing) and His eternality (always existing) makes it possible that in His foreknowledge He knew us.

Since we find no biblical support for #1, we'll address #2.

When God said *"before I formed you..."* He was clearly speaking of a beginning time for our existence. He placed that beginning as *"in the womb."* The text indicates that when God spoke of knowing us prior to our being formed, He was speaking of a foreknowledge that only He has. Foreknowledge does not support the idea of our preexistence, but only of God's pre-knowledge (before-knowledge) because only God is eternally existent.

God often spoke and gave revelation through His foreknowledge. Consider the prophecy given to Isaiah:

> *Isaiah 44:28 That saith of Cyrus, He is my shepherd, and shall perform all my pleasure: even saying to Jerusalem, Thou shalt be built; and to the temple, Thy foundation shall be laid.*

> *Isaiah 45:1 Thus saith the LORD to his anointed, to Cyrus, whose right hand I have holden, to subdue nations before him; and I will loose the loins of kings, to open before him the two leaved gates; and the gates shall not be shut;*

The prophet Isaiah died 150 years before Cyrus was born; and these words, given to Isaiah by the Lord, were written 200 years before Cyrus. That's an example of God's "knowing" Cyrus before he was formed in the womb, but it does not indicate that Cyrus preexisted in spirit form. God knew Cyrus through His perfect foreknowledge. God knew that Cyrus would one day be born and would fulfill all things of which He had spoken about him.

Because we do not have the foreknowledge of God, it is therefore impossible for us to completely understand His foreknowledge. Remember, God's foreknowledge is omniscient (all-knowing) and infallible (never wrong). Our knowledge is limited and subject to error. However, we can acquire some understanding by considering examples of foreknowledge that we might have experienced. An example would be having knowledge of a premeditated crime—a crime that is already planned to be committed, but has not yet occurred. That would be a type of foreknowledge, but it doesn't make the perpetrator a criminal, nor does the actual crime exist until it is committed. Our foreknowledge is fallible because circumstances could change that would prevent the crime from taking place.

God's foreknowledge is infallible, because He knows all things that will come to pass. If He declares something, it will, with all certainty, take place. Therefore our foreknowledge is not like God's.

So in Jeremiah 1:5 when God says, "*Before I formed you in the womb I knew you,* " we should feel very comfortable in understanding that God in His foreknowledge can speak about things that are yet to come into existence as if they are already existing.

There are many verses in the Bible that speak about God's foreknowledge and help us understand it. Prophets spoke of God's foreknowledge:

Isaiah 42:9 Behold, the former things are come to pass, and new things do I declare: before they spring forth I tell you of them.

Isaiah 46:10 Declaring the end from the beginning, and from ancient times the things that are not yet done, saying, My counsel shall stand, and I will do all my pleasure:

Daniel 2:28 But there is a God in heaven that revealeth secrets, and maketh known to the king Nebuchadnezzar what shall be in the latter days. Thy dream, and the visions of thy head upon thy bed, are these...

Jesus spoke of God's foreknowledge

Matthew 24:36 But of that day and hour knoweth no man, no, not the angels of heaven, but my Father only.

Paul made a clear statement about God's foreknowledge, when he said:

... God, who gives life to the dead and calls those things which do not exist as though they did...

(Romans 4:17)

If you believe what you like in the Gospel, and reject what you don't like, it is not the Gospel you believe, but yourself. — *St. Augustine*

Q. 12

Other than 2 Timothy 3:16, what are some answers for the Bible being God's Word?

When Paul wrote to Timothy saying, "All scripture is given by inspiration of God, and is profitable for doctrine, for reproof, for correction, for instruction in righteousness..." (2 Timothy 3:16), he was speaking of the Scripture that was already written at that time—what we call the Old Testament. Although that statement is also true of the New Testament Scriptures, it does not always serve as the best proof text for claiming that the New Testament is God-breathed. So how do we know that the New Testament writings are divinely inspired? Let's consider the biblical evidence and the many reasons that assure us that the Bible is God's divinely inspired and preserved Word.

The Gospels and the Book of Acts are actual historical accounts—records of events, places and people that can be supported by other historical documents. Paul also validates much of those books in his letters.

Let's address a few of the validations of the New Testament being God's Word.

Peter's Testimony

In referring to Paul's letters, Peter equated Paul's writing to Scripture when he wrote:

2 Peter 3:14-16 Therefore, beloved, looking forward to these things, be diligent to be found by Him in peace, without spot and blameless; and consider that the longsuffering of our Lord is salvation; as also our beloved brother Paul, according to the wisdom given to him, has written to you, as also in all his epistles, speaking in them of these things, in which are some things hard to understand, which untaught and unstable people twist to their own destruction, as they do also the rest of the Scriptures.

We know that Peter was selected and commissioned by Jesus to help build the Church, so it is noteworthy that he esteemed Paul's writings as accurate, authoritative *and* on par with "*the rest of the Scriptures.*"

It is unknown whether Paul ever thought his letters would be gathered and preserved for teaching purposes in the same way as the Hebrew Tanakh (Bible) was used for teaching. But we do know from historical documents that his letters were collectively used as early as the 2nd century for teaching in churches.

Paul's Apostolic and Spiritual Authority

We also know that Paul was taught by Jesus, which gave him apostolic authority:

Galatians 1:11-12 But I certify you, brethren, that the gospel which was preached of me is not after man. For I neither received it of man, neither was I taught it, but by the revelation of Jesus Christ.

Additionally, Paul claimed to be taught by the Holy Spirit:

1 Corinthians 2:9-13 But as it is written: "Eye has not seen, nor ear heard, Nor have entered into the heart of man The things which God has prepared for those who love Him." But God has revealed them to us through His Spirit. For the Spirit searches all things, yes, the deep things of God. For what man knows the things of a man except the spirit of the man which is in him? Even so no one knows the things of God except the Spirit of God. Now we have received, not the spirit of the world, but the Spirit who is from God, that we might know the

Some read the Bible to learn and some read the Bible to hear from heaven.
—Andrew Murray

things that have been freely given to us by God. These things we also speak, not in words which man's wisdom teaches but which the Holy Spirit teaches, comparing spiritual things with spiritual.

Understanding that Paul had both apostolic and spiritual authority gives us reason to believe that his writings are divinely inspired. Therefore we are to be "mindful of" his words just as we are of the prophets and all the apostles:

2 Peter 3:2 That ye may be mindful of the words which were spoken before by the holy prophets, and of the commandment of us the apostles of the Lord and Saviour:

Canonization of the Holy Scriptures

Another consideration is the careful and prayerful diligence of the early church fathers in their canonization of the Holy Bible. The word canon comes from a Greek word meaning rule or measuring stick. Study of the process of canonization reveals a meticulous methodology of determining the authority and authenticity of the books that make up our Holy Bible.

God's Promise

Finally, in offering proof of the authenticity of the New Testament as Scripture, we have God's faithful promise that He would preserve His Word.

Psalms 119:89 For ever, O LORD, thy word is settled in heaven.

Psalms 119:160 Thy word is true from the beginning: and every one of thy righteous judgments endureth for ever.

Psalms 119:152 Concerning thy testimonies, I have known of old that thou hast founded them for ever.

Proverbs 22:20-21 Have not I written to thee excellent things in counsels and knowledge, That I might make thee know the certainty of the words of truth; that thou mightest answer the words of truth to them that send unto thee?

> *Matthew 24:35 Heaven and earth shall pass away, but my words shall not pass away*

> *John 10:35 …the scripture cannot be broken;*

> *1 Peter 1:24-25 For all flesh is as grass, and all the glory of man as the flower of grass. The grass withereth, and the flower thereof falleth away: But the word of the Lord endureth for ever. And this is the word which by the gospel is preached unto you.*

God has told us we are to live by His Word.

> *Matthew 4:4 …He answered and said, It is written, Man shall not live by bread alone, but by every word that proceedeth out of the mouth of God.*

God would not have given us this command if He had not also preserved His Word. For it is by His Word that we can know His plan and purpose for our lives (what He desires *for* us) and our reasonable service to His will and ways (what He desires *from* us).

It ultimately comes down to trusting in the Word of God and the God of the Word. Do you trust God? He hasn't asked us to know or understand everything, but He does want us to believe His Word and to trust in Him always—and that means even when we might not fully understand something. Be patient and seek the Holy Spirit, for God has promised:

> *…when he, the Spirit of truth, is come, he will guide you into all truth: for he shall not speak of himself; but whatsoever he shall hear, that shall he speak: and he will show you things to come. He shall glorify me: for he shall receive of mine, and shall show it unto you.*
> *(John 16:13-14)*

Q. 13

Which Bible Translation is Best?

There are many Bible translations, and it should be a goal of the Church to continue working to have the Bible translated into every language. But what's implied in this question is, why are there so many English translations and which is best?

Why are there so many English translations?

There are numerous answers to that question. One reason is the challenges of translating from one language to another. A Hebrew or Greek word might not have an equivalent English word, or there might be more than one English word that conveys the meaning of the Hebrew or Greek word. Therefore, Bible translators make choices regarding which English word they believe best conveys the meaning of the word in the original language. That's a reason we find various translations using different words.

Another reason for so many English Bibles is because Bibles sell and publishing is a profitable industry. Especially today we see Bibles being published to meet personal preferences of the reader. There are women's Bibles, men's Bibles, students' Bibles, teens' Bibles, children's Bibles, etc. There are numerous study Bibles, each with a different focus or a varied commentary. There are Bibles that are very conservative in translation and those that are very liberal. And the list goes on and on.

Remember also that with every modern Bible translated and published there must be a copyright. In order to obtain a copyright the work must be original within specified standards. Therefore, changing enough words or phrases produces a manuscript that is different from others and can be copyrighted.

With an understanding of why there are so many English Bibles available today, let's address which one is best. Understanding manuscript evidence (i.e. the documents upon which the translation is based) helps to answer this question. That doesn't mean you must know Hebrew or Greek; rather that you have an understanding of the two different lines of translation and their differences.

The two lines of manuscript evidence are labeled by the city from which they originate. One line derives from Antioch, Syria and the other from Alexandria, Egypt.

From the Antioch manuscripts we have the following English translations (not an all inclusive list): Wycliffe Bible (1388), Tyndale Bible (1522), Coverdale Bible (1535), Matthews Bible (1537), Great Bible (1539), Geneva Bible (1560), Bishops Bible (1568), King James Bible (1611), and New King James Bible (1982)

From the Alexandrian manuscripts we have the following English translations (not an all inclusive list): Douay-Rheims (1582), Revised Version (1881), American Standard Version (1901), and many other more modern translations (RSV, NASV, LB, NSRB, JB, TEV, NEB, NIV, GNB, NRSV, NAB, NCV, NBV, HCSB, ISV, ESV).

There are significant translation differences between the two manuscript lines. It is a hotly debated topic which line is best, and it can only be decided after personal research and study.

Literal versus Dynamic Equivalent Translations

In addition to the two different manuscript lines, there are also differences in translation style. Literal translations are a word-for-word rendering of the Hebrew and Greek that strive to maintain the sentence structure and emphasis of the original language. Dynamic Equivalent translations are often called thought-for-thought translations, and they take more liberty and venture into the "gray area" between translation and interpretation.

Literal translations include the King James (KJV), New King James (NKJV), New American Standard (NASB), New English

Translation Bible (NET), Amplified Bible (AMP), Revised Standard (RSV) The Holman Christian Standard Bible (HCSB) and English Standard Versions (ESV).

Dynamic Equivalent translations include the New International Version (NIV), New American Bible (NAB), New English Bible (NEB), New Living Translation (NLT) and New Revised Standard (NRSV).

There is also another style of "translation" called free or paraphrase. It should be understood that these are not truly translations, but rather man's interpretation of the Bible and, in some cases, a re-wording of the Bible. The purpose of these works is to present a very readable interpretation of the Scriptures in modern English language. In these works some of the biblical accounts are rewritten in ways that have very little similarity to accounts found in literal or dynamic translations.

Free or paraphrase translations include the Living Bible (LB), Phillips Modern English (PME), Good News Bible (GNB), Modern Language (ML), Contemporary English (CEV), Today's English (TEV), Worldwide English (WEV) and The Message (MSG).

Should these free/paraphrase "translations" be avoided? Not necessarily. But it should be remembered that these paraphrases are not the actual Word of God. They are often a very loose interpretation of the Holy Scriptures and therefore should be read with the same caution needed when reading any book written by a Christian writer. Human writers are subject to much error. It is God's inspired Word alone that He has promised is both pure and preserved.

Psalms 12:6 The words of the LORD are pure words: as silver tried in a furnace of earth, purified seven times.

Psalms 119:140 Your word is very pure; Therefore Your servant loves it.

Proverbs 30:5 Every word of God is pure: he is a shield unto them that put their trust in him.

Matthew 24:35 Heaven and earth shall pass away, but my words shall not pass away.

John 10:35 ... and the scripture cannot be broken

1 Peter 1:23 Being born again, not of corruptible seed, but of incorruptible, by the word of God, which liveth and abideth for ever.

At Reasons for Hope*Jesus we primarily use the KJV and the NKJV. However, we believe that people can learn from any translation, because it is the Holy Spirit who teaches us.

John 14:26 But the Comforter, which is the Holy Ghost, whom the Father will send in my name, he shall teach you all things, and bring all things to your remembrance, whatsoever I have said unto you.

John 16:13 Howbeit when he, the Spirit of truth, is come, he will guide you into all truth: for he shall not speak of himself; but whatsoever he shall hear, that shall he speak: and he will show you things to come.

We encourage you to do your own research and come to your own conclusion before selecting which Bible you will read. Keep in mind the translation you choose will influence how you interpret verses and passages.

We recommend the use of a literal (word-for-word) translation for in-depth Bible study. For enjoyment, either a literal or dynamic equivalence is a good choice. Paraphrases can be used for additional understanding of passages in a more culturally contextual way, but just remember that paraphrases are no different than commentaries. They are man's interpretation.

Whatever Bible you select, spend time in the Word and grow in your knowledge and love of the Lord.

Grow in the grace and knowledge of our Lord and Savior Jesus Christ. To Him be the glory both now and forever. Amen. (2 Peter 3:18)

Q. 14

How do I cope when a loved one dies very young?

> *Blessed are they that mourn: for they shall be comforted.*
>
> *—Jesus Christ*

Loss of someone we love is never easy, regardless of their age. Their absence in our lives breaks our hearts and steals our joy.

Always allow time for grieving, understanding that we were created by God to feel emotions and that grieving is a natural process of coping with loss. God gave us the ability to love, and He has given us the ability to grieve. Remember also, we know and can trust that He is with us in our grief.

Yes, we grieve at the death of friends and family of all ages. We even grieve when we hear of the death of people we don't know, perhaps public figures we admire or deaths from violence or catastrophe. But let's consider the very specific loss of someone young—perhaps a child or a young adult.

As with all death, we should remember that God did not create us to suffer and die. He created Adam and Eve perfect, and it was only because of their disobedience that sin entered the world and the physical body became subject to death. They were banished from the Garden of Eden where they had been given the Tree of Life. No longer would their bodies be eternal. Of course we also know that along with the beginning of the process of a physical death came a spiritual death. But God in His mercy provided a way for man to be restored both spiritually and physically.

So, as Christians, we have great comfort when a loved one who belongs to the Lord dies. Because they were spiritually reborn and given eternal life with Christ, we know they are now with Him.

If we have lost someone whom we believe was not saved, we can still have hope that before they took their last breath they trusted in Christ. Remember it is Christ who saves. Even if we did not hear a public profession of faith, there is always hope that the person might have called out to Christ before taking their final breath. That may not give us the comfort we desire, but it does give us hope—a hope in Christ's mercy and grace.

Back to the question of dealing with the loss of a young person. It might be easier to accept the loss of the elderly because in our understanding they have lived a more complete and full life. We fully acknowledge that losing someone at a young age is often more difficult. But coping with the death of anyone we love, under any circumstances, should always be the same for Christians.

...we will stand amazed to see the topside of the tapestry and how God beautifully embroidered each circumstance into a pattern for our good and His glory.
— Joni Eareckson Tada

We must remember to do exactly what God commands—trust in Christ. He commands this because He loves us. We are to trust that He is the Sovereign God over everything, and in His purpose and plan He is working all things out for our good and His glory (Romans 8:28). Believe that even in our greatest losses are His blessings and His will for us in Christ Jesus (1 Thessalonians 5:18). Remember and believe that one day we will understand.

Allow yourself time to grieve. Let the heart break and the tears flow, but in doing so seek the Lord and He will give you His peace (John 14:27) and comfort (John 14:16-18). It might not seem to be enough at first, but trust in Christ's promises, and as you move forward you will feel His presence more and feel the pain of loss less.

I have personally experienced the loss of loved ones who were very young—two nephews at eight and nine, a best friend at 16, and a daughter at 29 (a prodigal loss—not death, but a similar experience of loss and pain). What comforted me most in each loss was very different. I was a child myself when my nephews drowned and it was my parents who explained that they were in Heaven and now living with Jesus. It was a very simple assurance of hope in God's promises for His people. When my best friend died at 16, all of us (her girlfriends) were inconsolable at her funeral. It was her mother who came to us and comforted us with the words, "don't cry for Jill, she's with her Lord and Saviour in Heaven." Those are words I've never forgotten. Her mother's words were a powerful testimony to a group of teenage girls. What honor and glory she brought to the Lord with her words. Both of these examples provided an eternal perspective and gave comfort from the promises of Jesus. We know that Jesus has prepared a place for us and one day we will go to be with Him.

There were many other losses of gone-too-soon friends and family—a childhood playmate from illness, a long-time friend who drowned in college, a nephew by suicide, a great-nephew killed in a car accident, a best friend from college who lost his battle to cancer, a cousin who was murdered... and far too many others.

In the most painful loss I have ever experienced (loss of relationship with someone I love), I came to understand how important the mind is in the grieving process. By continually remembering who God is, what He has done for me and who I am in Christ, I found the strength, comfort and rest I needed. Although it may be different than a loss by death, a loss of relationship brings similar pain and suffering. When someone we love dearly is no longer in our lives, it leaves a void. Of course we know that God can restore relationships, but sometimes He chooses not to do so. When we suffer, He never tells us to just get over it; rather, He promises to be with us and to bring us through the pain and suffering of loss.

...Sometimes the Lord calms the storm.

Sometimes He lets the storm rage and calms His child.

Whether God takes someone out of our lives by His providential or His permissive will, whether it's by death or by separation, we can rest in Christ's faithfulness and trust that He will fill the void with more of Himself. While we still may feel the loss deeply, when we find our comfort and rest in Christ we no longer feel it so desperately.

I speak about this in my book *Why the Butterfly? Rightly Remembering Jesus*. Rightly remembering those three things (who God is, what He has done for us and who we are in Christ) focuses our minds and hearts on Jesus. Rightly remembering will help us to have an eternal perspective. And, by anchoring our hope in Jesus, we can transform our minds and cope with grief much better.

So again, it is important to allow yourself time to grieve and it is important to direct your mind, your will and your emotions during the grieving process.

A Biblical Process to Heal the Heart and Refresh the Soul

Prayer honors God, acknowledges His being, exalts His power, adores His providence, secures His aid. —E.M. Bounds

1) Seek the Lord first. Pour out your heart to the Lord in prayer and hear Him speak to you through His Word. Read the Bible focusing on His provision of comfort and peace in your suffering. Remember that Jesus wept when His friend Lazarus died (John 11:35). Shed your tears and experience the pain, but in your grief look for the Lord's blessings. Laura Story puts it well in the refrain from her song, *Blessings*:

What if your blessings come through rain drops
What if Your healing comes through tears
What if a thousand sleepless nights
are what it takes to know You're near
What if trials of this life are Your mercies in disguise

2) Allow your Christian friends to comfort you. When the grief is so great you can't see the Light through the tears and you can't find His joy in your pain, let God work through His children. God will use your brothers and sisters in Christ to minister to you and to share His love and His promises with you.

3) Have an eternal perspective. Life in a fallen world was not what God intended for us. With all its pain and suffering, this earth is not our home. There is a home of total peace and comfort promised to us by Jesus (John 14). The song, *Turn Your Eyes Upon Jesus* (Helen H. Lemmel, 1922), reminds us of this hope:

Turn your eyes upon Jesus
Look full, in his wonderful face
And the things of earth will grow strangely dim
In the light of his glory and grace

Remember, one day God will wipe away every tear. God will make all things new.

> *And God shall wipe away all tears from their eyes; and there shall be no more death, neither sorrow, nor crying, neither shall there be any more pain: for the former things are passed away. (Revelation 21:4)*

God will mend a broken heart if you give Him all the pieces.

But until that day...

May the God of hope fill you with all joy and peace in believing, that you may abound in hope by the power of the Holy Spirit. (Romans 15:13)

*Jesus

The wisdom of God devised a way for the love of God to deliver sinners from the wrath of God while not compromising the righteousness of God.

— *John Piper*

Q. 15

Was Jesus a sacrifice to Satan to free us from Satan so God could save us?

We know that Jesus gave Himself as a sacrifice for our sin, but was the sacrifice made *to* Satan?

> *Galatians 1:4 Who* [Jesus] *gave himself for our sins, that he might deliver us from this present evil world, according to the will of God and our Father:*

The sacrifice of Jesus was to satisfy God's justice and to free us from the penalty and power of sin.

Jesus satisfied God's justice.

God is a just God and He will judge sin. He created us to be in perfect communion with Him and when Adam disobeyed God sin entered the world. Now all people are born with the sin of Adam.

> *Romans 5:12 Therefore, just as through one man sin entered the world, and death through sin, and thus death spread to all men, because all sinned.*

It is God's desire to restore His creation to Himself. Jesus made that possible by taking upon Himself our sin, paying the penalty for it and imputing (crediting) His righteousness to all who would come to believe in Him.

> *2 Corinthians 5:21 For he hath made him to be sin for us, who knew no sin; that we might be made the righteousness of God in him.*

When we repent and trust in Christ's finished work on the cross we are washed in His blood and made righteous. Therefore, when we stand before God, we are acceptable in His eyes.

Revelation 1:5 And from Jesus Christ, who is the faithful witness, and the first begotten of the dead, and the prince of the kings of the earth. Unto him that loved us, and washed us from our sins in his own blood...

Romans 3:21-22 ...now the righteousness of God without the law is manifested, being witnessed by the law and the prophets; Even the righteousness of God which is by faith of Jesus Christ unto all and upon all them that believe...

Jesus freed us from the penalty of sin.

We just spoke of God's justice. In His justice, God required that sin be judged and the penalty for it be paid. Jesus paid that penalty. Our sins were laid on Him and God judged sin. Jesus' pure [sinless] blood was the atonement (payment price) for our sins.

Isaiah 53:6 All we like sheep have gone astray; we have turned every one to his own way; and the LORD hath laid on him the iniquity of us all.

2 Corinthians 5:21 For he hath made him to be sin for us...

1 Peter 2:24 Who his own self bare our sins in his own body on the tree, that we, being dead to sins, should live unto righteousness: by whose stripes ye were healed.

Jesus freed us from the power of sin.

For those who trust in Christ's work on the cross and have received Him as Lord and Saviour, Jesus has not only saved us from the penalty of sin, He has also saved us from the power of sin. This doesn't mean we will never sin again. It means, by His Spirit, we have been given power to overcome sin and to live in victory.

1 John 5:4 For whatsoever is born of God overcometh the world: and this is the victory that overcometh the world, even our faith.

We have been given His power to choose not to sin; but, since we are not yet freed from the presence of sin, we all too often choose poorly. We fight against the three things described in 1 John 2:16: the lust of the flesh (our own sin nature and sinful desires), the lust of the eyes (the deception of the world that lures us into sin) and the pride of life (finding satisfaction in ourselves rather than in Christ).

It was pride that changed angels into devils; it is humility that makes men as angels.
— Saint Augustine

Additionally, we have not yet been freed from the presence or power of Satan. Satan and his minions are still present in our world and are still at work doing what they desire to do...tempting us to sin. Again, always remember that when Jesus saved us He gave us the gift of the Person and power of the Holy Spirit.

> *John 14:16-17 And I will pray the Father, and he shall give you another Comforter, that he may abide with you for ever; Even the Spirit of truth; whom the world cannot receive, because it seeth him not, neither knoweth him: but ye know him; for he dwelleth with you, and shall be in you.*

> *1 John 4:4 Ye are of God, little children, and have overcome them: because greater is he that is in you, than he that is in the world.*

Jesus was not a sacrifice to free us from Satan. We never belonged to him. Everything in this world belongs to God.

> *Psalm 24:1 A Psalm of David. The earth is the LORD'S, and the fulness thereof; the world, and they that dwell therein.*

> *1 Corinthians 10:26 For the earth is the Lord's, and the fullness thereof.*

In summary, Jesus' atoning death was to satisfy God's justice, to save us from God's punishment of sin and to make reconciliation to God possible for all who trust in His finished work on the cross.

Share this amazing gift with someone today!!!

*Jesus

Reader Response to *Was Jesus a Sacrifice to Satan?*

(readers comments designated as KP*; mine as* SA*)*

Dear Ms Abbott:

KP: *I enjoyed your article in answer to the question "Was Jesus a sacrifice to free us from Satan? Yet verses came to mind that I would like your comments on.*

When Jesus was in the desert and was tempted by the devil, the devil offered him the kingdoms of the world and all the glory, if he would bow down and worship him. Jesus did not correct the devil because he had spoken correctly. The kingdoms of this world were delivered into the hands of the devil when Adam sinned.

> *Matthew 4:8 Again, the devil taketh him up into an exceeding high mountain, and sheweth him all the kingdoms of the world, and the glory of them;*

> *Luke 4:5-6 And the devil, taking him up into an high mountain, shewed unto him all the kingdoms of the world in a moment of time. And the devil said unto him, All this power will I give thee, and the glory of them: for that is delivered unto me; and to whomsoever I will I give it.*

+++

SA: Satan *did* claim to be able to give to Jesus all the "power" and "glory" of the kingdoms of the world. And yes, we know that Satan is the "prince of this world" (John 12:31, 14:30, 16:11), but his control is only to the extent that God allows. Remember, God is sovereign over everything. An example is that Satan was unable to afflict Job without God allowing it. Satan claimed that he would give "all this power" and "the glory of [the kingdoms]" to Jesus, but we know Satan has been lying since the beginning. Remember he said, *"ye shall not surely die...ye shall be as gods..."* (Genesis 3:3-4).

Did Satan truly have the ability to give the power and glory of the kingdoms of this world to Jesus? He didn't own them:

> *Psalm 24:1 A Psalm of David. The earth is the LORD'S, and the fulness thereof; the world, and they that dwell therein.*

If Satan was offering to cease his influence over them, then yes he could have done that. But that also would have meant he was surrendering to Jesus. So perhaps what we read in Matthew 4 and Luke 4 is Satan doing what he does best—trying to deceive with a lie just as he did in the Garden.

Note that Jesus did not address the kingdoms of this world, confirming or denying whether Satan was able to give them to Him. Instead, Jesus only responded by quoting Scripture:

> *Matthew 4:10 Then saith Jesus unto him, Get thee hence, Satan: for it is written, Thou shalt worship the Lord thy God, and him only shalt thou serve.*

Satan was clearly serving himself when he made this offer, but it does not give reason to support that Jesus' death was in any way a payment to Satan .

+++

KP: *Also what comes to mind are verses that speak of our having been captive.*

> *Ephesians 4:8 Wherefore he saith, When he ascended up on high, he led captivity captive, and gave gifts unto men.*

> *2 Timothy 2:26 And that they may recover themselves out of the snare of the devil, who are taken captive by him at his will.*

> *Luke 4:18 The Spirit of the Lord is upon me, because he hath anointed me to preach the gospel to the poor; he hath sent me to heal the brokenhearted, to preach deliverance to the captives...*

+++

SA: "Captivity" does not mean we belong to Satan. We are captive to many things. You correctly mention two—sin and death. The captivity that Satan has over non-believers, or believers, takes place when man falls prey, or captive, to his will. This captivity is a type of power he has over us, but it's not a possession of us. Consider an American citizen who is imprisoned in a hostile foreign country. That country holds the person captive, but the person does not belong to that country. Their citizenship remains American. So also our citizenship is in Heaven and therefore we belong to God. Again, Psalm 24 clearly tells that all of creation belongs to God, not Satan.

Psalm 24:1 A Psalm of David. The earth is the LORD'S, and the fulness thereof; the world, and they that dwell therein.

We are told to bring " into captivity every thought to the obedience of Christ" (2 Corinthians 10:5). That would certainly diminish Satan's captivity over us.

+++

KP: *I appreciated your pointing out that we must submit to God and resist the devil and he will flee from us and that this is an ongoing war against spiritual principalities as the Scriptures note.*

Ephesians 6:12 For we wrestle not against flesh and blood, but against principalities, against powers, against the rulers of the darkness of this world, against spiritual wickedness in high places.

But doesn't this verse inform us that without Christ man is captive by the deceit of lack of knowledge of the truth?

Ephesians 2:2 Wherein in time past ye walked according to the course of this world, according to the prince of the power of the air, the spirit that now worketh in the children of disobedience:

+++

SA: Keep in mind that the Ephesians verses are written to believers to say that we do "wrestle" against such things, and in the past we "walked according" to such things. Yes, these are types of captivity—lack of knowledge, the course of this world and Satan. But captivity is not the same as ownership. Remember the original question in it's entirety:

> *Was Jesus a human sacrifice TO Satan, to free you from Satan so God can save you?*

Satan does not own us, so Jesus' death was not a sacrifice TO Satan as a type of purchase price. Jesus' death had nothing to do with freeing us from Satan's power SO THAT God could save us. His death paid the penalty for our sin, and appeased the requirement of a just Judge. It was not any type of payment to Satan.

+++

KP: *When Adam disobeyed God in the Garden, didn't he also at that time transfer his jurisdiction over to the devil as the exchange with Jesus indicates? So then the dominion that God had given Adam was then delivered to the devil who is said to be the god of this world?*

+++

SA: It depends on what you mean by "jurisdiction." When Adam sinned, he broke the perfect communion he had with God, he died spiritually and his body began to die physically. Adam was cast out of the place that God had prepared for him to live (similar to how Satan rebelled against God and was cast down from Heaven). Again, true dominion (and jurisdiction) belongs to God. The dictionary defines dominion as: the power or right of governing and controlling; sovereign authority. These verses proclaim that true dominion (sovereign authority) belongs to God.

> *Deuteronomy 10:14 Indeed heaven and the highest heavens belong to the LORD your God, also the earth with all that is in it.*

> *Psalm 50:10-12 For every beast of the forest is mine, and the cattle upon a thousand hills. I know all the fowls of the moun-*

tains: and the wild beasts of the field are mine. If I were hungry, I would not tell thee: for the world is mine, and the fullness thereof.

Psalm 104:24 O LORD, how manifold are Your works! In wisdom You have made them all. The earth is full of Your possessions...

1 Chronicles 29:11 Yours, O LORD, is the greatness, The power and the glory, The victory and the majesty; For all that is in heaven and in earth is Yours; Yours is the kingdom, O LORD, And You are exalted as head over all.

+++

KP: *Didn't Jesus proclaim that the kingdom of God is not "of this world" but is within those who follow after Him?*

+++

SA: Yes, Jesus did say that (Matthew 18:36). The Kingdom He speaks of in Matthew 18:36 is a spiritual kingdom. It is the Kingdom of God that unites all those who have repented, trusted in Jesus' finished work on the cross for the payment of their sins, and have received Him as Lord. Just as Hebrews 11:13 proclaims the Old Testament Saints to be *"strangers and pilgrims on earth,"* we are also pilgrims in this earthly, worldly kingdom. Our citizenship is in a spiritual kingdom (Philippians 3:20) and our King is on the throne in Heaven. Yet, even this earthly, worldly kingdom belongs to God. He is Sovereign over all.

+++

KP: *I think your article is very helpful but I am not convinced from your answer that we did not need a hostage exchange of sorts, being that all are born "dead."*

Ephesians 2:1 And you hath he quickened, who were dead in trespasses and sins;

Colossians 2:13 And you, being dead in your sins and the uncircumcision of your flesh, hath he quickened together with him, having forgiven you all trespasses;

Colossians 1:13 Who hath delivered us from the power of darkness, and hath translated us into the kingdom of his dear Son:

+++

SA: The Bible does not teach any type of "hostage exchange." Yes, we are born dead in our sins. But the death of Jesus was not a "sacrifice *TO* Satan" as a "hostage exchange." It was an atoning sacrifice to pay for our sins. It was God who was satisfied by this sacrifice, not Satan. (remember the original question—a "sacrifice TO Satan"). Again, we don't *belong* to Satan, so our deliverance is not *from* Satan. Our deliverance is from the penalty of sin, death and the *power* of Satan.

+++

KP: *We are "translated" from the "power of darkness" of this world ....that jurisdiction that the devil deceived Adam into making. Adam made a free choice to disobey with knowledge... then all died in Adam .*

1 Corinthians 15:22 For as in Adam all die, even so in Christ shall all be made alive.

+++

SA: Three points you make that I would like to address:

1) I agree that we are "translated from the power of darkness." The key word is "power." The original question was about whether Satan had possession of us and so a sacrifice was made to him. While He did have power over us, he did not own us. If that were the case, he could have refused to accept a payment. I maintain that Scripture teaches everything belongs to God (see verses on page 91).

2) Satan deceived Eve, but not Adam. Adam was not deceived, he sinned knowingly.

> *2 Corinthians 11:3 ...he serpent beguiled Eve through his subtlety.*

> *1 Timothy 2:14 ... Adam was not deceived, but the woman being deceived was in the transgression.*

3) The Bible doesn't speak of a transfer of "jurisdiction" from Adam to Satan. Adam had dominion over the Garden in which God placed him. When Adam sinned, he was cast out into a world that God never intended for him—one in which sin would abound, one in which he would not have the dominion which God had intended.

Yes, Satan is the "prince of this world," but, as we see in Job, his powers are limited. Just as Adam was given dominion (authority) to do God's will, we also are given power (authority) to do God's will. We are given the Holy Spirit who works in and through us to accomplish God's good will.

+++

KP: *I think the operative key word here is "in." Those who are "in Christ"....have then passed from the death that we are born into this world ...the flesh being dead without the spirit. Thus we must be found "in Christ" wherein is life, and life eternal. In Jesus Christ we are passed from death...unto life.*

> *John 5:24 Verily, verily, I say unto you, He that heareth my word, and believeth on him that sent me, hath everlasting life, and shall not come into condemnation; but is passed from death unto life.*

Thank you for your time and effort to read this to give an answer to bring some more light on this issue.

Respectfully His, KP

SA: That's a beautiful summation of saving grace in Christ. Thanks for closing this discussion with God's beautiful promise of life eternal *in* the Lord Jesus Christ.

In His Service, Shari Abbott

The Rest of the Story

After posting our dialogue, KP responded again, saying:

I appreciated your reply ...I realized that I missed the word "TO" in the title just as you noted later on! How important it is to take heed to the "little" word. So much in Scripture hinges on words like "and, but," and (in this case) "TO."

In my response to KP, I mentioned an Internet forward with a story that has perpetuated the idea of our being purchased back from Satan. KP had not seen the article, so perhaps many of you have also not seen it (and that's a good thing). I'd like to share this story with you, so you can be aware of the heresy it teaches. Sadly, this Internet forward has been widely circulated.

The story begins on the next page and it is from Paul Harvey's radio show, *The Rest of the Story.* Paul Harvey's show aired morning, noon and mid-day on stations across the country from the 1950s-1990s. His programs reached as many as 24 million people each week.

The story that follows is not biblically correct, and I will address that at the end. We should, however, note that it is well documented that Paul Harvey (1918-2009) was a Christian, and therefore he is now in Heaven with the Lord. We have every reason to believe that Paul Harvey did not understand the false teachings in the story that he shared. Read carefully this touching story and see if you can discern the unbiblical teaching.

The Bird Cage

There once was a man named George Thomas, a pastor in a small New England town. One Easter Sunday morning he came to the church carrying a rusty, bent, old bird cage, and set it by the pulpit. Several eyebrows were raised and, as if in response, Pastor Thomas began to speak.

"I was walking through town yesterday when I saw a young boy coming toward me, swinging this bird cage. On the bottom of the cage were three little wild birds, shivering with cold and fright. I stopped the boy and asked, "What you got there son?"

"Just some old birds," came the reply.

"What are you gonna do with them?" I asked.

"Take 'em home and have fun with 'em. I'm gonna tease 'em and pull out their feathers to make 'em fight. I'm gonna have a real good time."

"But you'll get tired of those birds sooner or later. What will you do then?"

"Oh, I got some cats. They like birds. I'll take 'em to them."

The pastor was silent for a moment. "How much do you want for those birds, son?"

"Huh? Why, you don't want them birds, mister. They're just plain old field birds. They don't sing – they ain't even pretty!"

"How much?" The boy sized up the pastor as if he were crazy and said,

"$10?"

The pastor reached in his pocket and took out a ten dollar bill. He placed it in the boy's hand. In a flash, the boy was gone. The pastor picked up the cage and gently carried it to the end of the alley where there was a tree and a grassy spot. Setting the cage down, he opened the door, and by softly tapping the bars persuaded the birds to fly out, setting them free.

Well, that explained the empty bird cage on the pulpit, and then the pastor began to tell this story.

One day Satan and Jesus were having a conversation. Satan had just come from the Garden of Eden, and he was gloating and boasting.

"Yes, sir, I just caught the world full of people down there. Set me a trap, used bait I knew they couldn't resist. Got 'em all!"

"What are you going to do with them?" Jesus asked.

"Oh, I'm gonna have fun! I'm gonna teach them how to marry and divorce each other. How to hate and abuse each other. How to drink and smoke and curse. How to invent guns and bombs and kill each other. I'm really gonna have fun!"

"And what will you do when you get done with them?" Jesus asked.

"Oh, I'll kill 'em."

"How much do you want for them?"

"Oh, you don't want those people. They ain't no good. Why, you'll take them and they'll just hate you. They'll spit on you, curse you and kill you!! You don't want those people!!"

"How much?"

Satan looked at Jesus and sneered, "Your life."

Jesus paid the price.

The pastor picked up the cage, opened the door and he walked from the pulpit.

+++

Do you understand the errors in this message? First, a conversation like this never took place. We have no record of any such discussion between Jesus and Satan and we are not at liberty to attribute such words to either of them. We are clearly told it is a sin to add to the words of God, and that includes in our minds as well as on the pages of a Bible translation.

Second, Jesus didn't give His life to redeem us from Satan. Jesus gave His life to pay the penalty for our sins. It is God the Father who judges sin. Jesus took our sin upon Himself and the cup of the wrath of God's indignation (God's cup of judgment) was poured out on Jesus. Jesus' death satisfied the Father, not Satan.

Be cautious with Internet forwards. While they are often touching and tell heartwarming stories, if they are not biblically accurate, they are heresy (a belief or opinion contrary to biblical doctrine). Be cautious to read and listen carefully, and to check what you hear and read against God's Word. Do not allow man's words, however touching and heartwarming they might be, to contradict what God has told us in the Bible.

Be like the people of Berea, who Paul talked about in the Bible. They listened to the Word of God spoken by man but searched the Scriptures to verify that what they were hearing was in accordance with what God says.

> *These* [the Bereans] *were more noble than those in Thessalonica, in that they received the word with all readiness of mind, and searched the scriptures daily, whether those things were so. Therefore many of them believed... (Acts 17:11-12)*

Q. 16

When is it OK to lie?

Q. Rahab lied when the army in Jericho asked her if the spies were in her house and yet she found favor with God. So when is it OK to lie?

It is never OK to lie. Lying is clearly defined as sinful by God. The prohibition of lying is the fourth of the ten commandments given in Exodus and reiterated in Deuteronomy and Leviticus:

Exodus 20:16 Thou shalt not bear false witness against thy neighbour.

Deuteronomy 5:20 Neither shalt thou bear false witness against thy neighbour.

Leviticus 19:11 Ye shall not steal, neither deal falsely, neither lie one to another.

...let your 'Yes' be 'Yes,' and your 'No,' 'No.'
— Jesus Christ

So Rahab's lie was a sin—and the fact that she found favor with God, does not in any way minimize her sin. It should, however, cause us to think of what a merciful and gracious God we have.

God was merciful in not punishing Rahab's sin. Everyone can point to sins they have committed that God has not punished. God's favor/blessings/grace is truly unmerited. It's not given because of what we do, but because of who God is. He is loving, merciful and gracious.

Critics of the Bible like to use the story of Rahab to say that God morally contradicted Himself by not judging and punishing Rahab's sin and instead blessing her and her family. They suggest that God approved of her lie because there was a good outcome.

Rahab found unmerited favor in God's eyes. God preserved her life because He had a plan and a purpose for her life and she had demonstrated a faith that would fuel her service to Him. It was not that God had blessed her when she sinned or had diminished her sin in any way, it was that God knew her heart and her faith...and God gave her mercy and grace.

Let's take a look at the historical account to better understand the reasons why critics are wrong.

The story of Rahab begins when Joshua sent two messengers (spies) into the city of Jericho to "view the land" prior to their moving forward in conquest to take the land (Joshua 2). The king was informed of the presence of the Israelite men and sent his men to require that Rahab turn them over. Rahab, however, hid the spies and lied, saying that she did not know where they were (Joshua 2:4). The men were then able to escape.

Faith is to believe what we do not see, and the reward of this faith is to see what we believe.
— Saint Augustine

We've established that Rahab *did* lie in this situation. But let's take a closer look at her words to the two messengers/spies. What she said clearly showed the condition of her heart and her faith in the God of Israel:

> *Joshua 2:9-11 and* [Rahab] *said to the men: "I know that the LORD has given you the land, that the terror of you has fallen on us, and that all the inhabitants of the land are fainthearted because of you. For we have heard how the LORD dried up the water of the Red Sea for you when you came out of Egypt, and what you did to the two kings of the Amorites who were on the*

other side of the Jordan, Sihon and Og, whom you utterly destroyed. And as soon as we heard these things, our hearts melted; neither did there remain any more courage in anyone because of you, for the LORD your God, He is God in heaven above and on earth beneath..."

We also read that she asked for deliverance for herself and her family in return for the protection she provided them:

Joshua 2:12-13 "Now therefore, I beg you, swear to me by the LORD, since I have shown you kindness, that you also will show kindness to my father's house, and give me a true token, and spare my father, my mother, my brothers, my sisters, and all that they have, and deliver our lives from death."

The men promised kindness if she would not disclose their whereabouts.

The Gospel is good news of mercy to the undeserving. The symbol of the religion of Jesus is the cross, not the scales. —John Stott

Joshua 2:14-15 So the men answered her, "Our lives for yours, if none of you tell this business of ours. And it shall be, when the LORD has given us the land, that we will deal kindly and truly with you." Then she let them down by a rope through the window, for her house was on the city wall; she dwelt on the wall.

Rahab and her family were spared when Israel sieged Jericho because of God's mercy and grace. She trusted in God enough to put her life at risk, demonstrating faith in the God of Israel. The Bible commends her faith in Hebrews 11:31.

By faith the harlot Rahab did not perish with those who did not believe, when she had received the spies with peace.

Note that Rahab *"did not perish with those who did not believe."* She was not among the unbelievers. She believed. She sheltered the spies and then *"sent them out another way"* (James 2:25).

The answer to the question, "when is it OK to lie?" is "never." In the account of Rahab's lie to protect the messengers, we see God's mercy demonstrated and His grace magnified. He forgave her sin and spared her and her family, not because of what she did to protect the spies, but because of her faith. She knew of the God of Israel, His mighty power and His giving of the land to Israel, and therefore had a fear and reverence of God. It was demonstrated by her act of offering aid and protection to the messengers.

God can forgive any sin. He can overlook none. —Billy Graham

Two additional points of interest about Rahab are found in the New Testament.

1) Rahab is never referred to as a liar. Her sin of lying was not overlooked—but it was forgiven.

2) God had a wonderful purpose and plan for Rahab, for in the genealogy of Jesus Christ we find Rahab included in the messianic line (Matthew 1:5).

But I have trusted in thy mercy; my heart shall rejoice in thy salvation. (Psalm 13:5)

For as the heaven is high above the earth, so great is his mercy toward them that fear him. (Psalm 103:11)

The LORD taketh pleasure in them that fear him, in those that hope in his mercy. (Psalm 147:11)

Salmon begat Boaz of Rahab,
and Boaz begat Obed of Ruth,
and Obed begat Jesse, and
Jesse begat David the king.
David the king begat Solomon...
(Matthew 1:5-6)

Q. 17

Saturday or Sunday Sabbath?

Q. I have been surfing the web and came across a church group that believes the resurrection was on the Sabbath (Saturday) and that worship of Jesus or His resurrection on Sunday, or any other day, is sinfully wrong and can be a determining factor in salvation. Please help me with this!

> *If you do not worship God seven days a week, you do not worship Him on one day a week. There is no such thing known in heaven as Sunday worship unless it is accompanied by Monday worship, Tuesday worship, and so on. — A.W. Tozer*

So this church says that gathering to worship Jesus on any day other than Saturday is sinful and is a determining factor in salvation? How sad that they would believe and teach this. There's no biblical support for it and such a belief is contrary to the gospel message of freedom and rest found in Christ.

Our day of corporate worship as a determining factor in our salvation is completely unbiblical. Our salvation is a free gift, unmerited and unearned by us, determined only by His goodness, mercy and grace. It is received by us when we repent and trust in His finished work upon the cross for the forgiveness of our sins.

Certainly we should gather to worship Jesus, but it can be done on any day of the week. The Bible is clear that God designated the seventh day of the week, Saturday, as the Sabbath day of rest for Israel (Exodus 20:8, Deuteronomy 5:12). Now, since Jesus' life, death, burial and resurrection, Jesus is our Sabbath rest (Hebrews 4). Our rest no longer comes *from* a designated day, but rather *in* a designated Person…the Lord Jesus Christ. We now find our sabbath rest in Him—and our rest in Him is now every day of the week. It is continual, without ceasing. We abide and rest in the richness of the gifts He has given us—our eternal life and His Spirit who teaches and guides us.

Gathering for fellowship and worship can be any day of the week. Therefore, Sunday is a perfectly acceptable day of worship, and since the first century AD it has been the traditional day for Christian worship.

It was mentioned that this church believes Jesus' resurrection was on a Saturday. That's a completely different topic, and I can only briefly address it here. A Saturday resurrection is held by those who believe Jesus was crucified on a Wednesday. They refer to Scripture that says "on the third day," and they count three literal 24 hour periods—starting with Wednesday afternoon to Thursday (1st day), Thursday-Friday (2nd day) and Friday-Saturday (3rd day). That means that Jesus had to rise from the dead before sundown on Saturday. While this might seem to make sense, Jesus spoke of both the days and nights:

> *Matthew 12:40 For as Jonas was three days and three nights in the whale's belly; so shall the Son of man be three days and three nights in the heart of the earth.*

A Wednesday crucifixion has four days (Wed, Thurs, Fri, Sat) and three nights (Wed, Thurs, Fri). That doesn't agree with what Jesus said. There are many other problems with a Wednesday crucifixion, but that's a topic for another time.

Again, remember, our sabbath rest is in a Person, the Lord Jesus Christ, not a day. Our corporate worship of Him can take place on any day, and our personal communion with Him should take place every day! For a more in-depth understanding of our rest in Jesus,

I am sharing this excerpt from *Remember Me – A Course in Rightly Remembering.* By understanding and keeping in remembrance who God is, what He has done for us and who we are in Christ, we find rest in Christ. For more information about the study course see page 169 of this book.

Remember the sabbath day, to keep it holy.

(from *Remember Me – A Course in Rightly Remembering*)

It's interesting to note that the first three of the Ten Commandments pertain to our relationship with the Lord, and the last six to our relationship with our fellow man. So where does the fourth commandment fit in?

Love is to the heart what the summer is to the farmer's year. It brings to harvest all the loveliest flowers of the soul. Indeed, it is the loveliest flower in the garden of God's grace.
— Billy Graham

The fourth commandment, *Remember the sabbath day, to keep it holy* (Exodus 20:8), is the one that binds the others together. It is the commandment to rest in God, and to find our satisfaction and peace in Him alone.

In His earthly incarnation, Jesus summarized the Ten Commandments with two Great Commandments:

> *Matthew 22:37-40 Thou shalt love the Lord thy God with all thy heart, and with all thy soul, and with all thy mind. This is the first and great commandment. And the second is like unto it, Thou shalt love thy neighbour as thyself. On these two commandments hang all the law and the prophets.*

The first three of the Ten Commandments are clearly summarized in the first and great commandment, and the last six are summarized in Jesus' second commandment. Jesus clearly proclaimed that the Law is all about love—loving God first and then your neighbor. But what about the fourth commandment?

If Jesus' first commandment is our vertical relationship and His second is our horizontal relationship, where is the commandment about the Sabbath?

Jesus Himself embodies the fourth commandment. Jesus is our Sabbath rest (Hebrews 4). He is our rest and His Law is love.

We are to abide in Christ and allow His love and His Spirit to work in and through us, and direct and guide us.

Abiding in Christ is our source of peace and comfort.

Abiding in Christ is our source of strength.

Abiding in Christ fuels us with His love.

Abiding in Christ enables us to love others.

Live your life in the light of what Jesus has done for you, and anchored in who He is and who you are in Him. [1]

It is Finished!

The heart is restless, 'till it rests in Thee. — Saint Augustine

1 Excerpted from *Remember Me–A Course in Rightly Remembering.* A companion study course to the book *Why the Butterfly? Rightly Remembering Jesus.*

Q. 18

What does it mean to be a "child of God?"

This question points us to some of the most beautiful verses in the Bible that contain precious promises of the loving, nurturing and protecting nature of God as our Father. We are promised that in Christ we are children of the Most High God:

John 1:12 But as many as received Him, to them He gave the right to become ***children of God*** *to those who believe in His name .*

Let's remember that when we repent and trust in Christ's finished work on the cross for the payment of our sins, we are born again by God's Spirit. And even more than an earthly father, our Heavenly Father loves us and nurtures us—for His love is a perfect love.

> *If I find in myself a desire which no experience in this world can satisfy, the most probable explanation is that I was made for another world. — C. S. Lewis*

Galatians 3:26 For ye are all the children of God by faith in Christ Jesus.

We become children of God by a heavenly adoption:

Romans 8:14-16 For as many as are led by the Spirit of God, they are the sons of God. For ye have not received the spirit of bondage again to fear; but ye have received the Spirit of adoption, whereby we cry, Abba, Father. The Spirit itself beareth witness with our spirit, that we are the children of God.

And with God as our Father, we become "joint-heirs" with Christ and *"heirs according to the promise:"*

Romans 8:17 And if children, then heirs; heirs of God, and joint-heirs with Christ; if so be that we suffer with him, that we may be also glorified together.

Galatians 3:29 And if ye be Christ's, then are ye Abraham's seed, and heirs according to the promise.

So what does this mean? It means that we have been given *all* that Christ has, in and with the Father. Session Six of the *Remember Me* study teaches about John 17 as the Last Will and Testament of Jesus Christ and about the precious promises we have been given. In John 17 we find the most intimate expression of Jesus' relationship with God the Father and we get the most precious insights into the unity and blessings of that relationship. The video study session reveals seven things Jesus bequeathed prior to His death.

Eternal life with Him (John 17:2, 24)
His Word (John 17:8, 14)
His Joy (John 17:13)
His mission (John 17:18)
His glory for unity with Him (John 17:22)
His love and presence (John 17:26)
His peace (John 14:27)

The Bible also provides promises and assurance that these gifts are given to us and that He has sealed His promises and our souls forevermore by His Spirit. The *Remember Me* John 17 study also tells of the witnesses to the will, the seal and the executor of the will and the responsibilities of the executor.[2]

Rejoice in the assurance that God is our Father and we are His children. His love is steadfast and our eternal destiny is secure.

Live your life to bring honor and glory to the One who gave His life so you could become a child of God.

Share your joy with others and proclaim the saving grace found only in Jesus Christ.

Let the Holy Spirit lead you and guide you, so one day you will hear, *"well done my good and faithful servant."*(Matthew 25:21)

Our purpose in this life is to honor and glorify God. (Isaiah 43:7, Revelation 4:11)

Our goal is to be conformed to the image of Jesus Christ. (Romans 8:29)

Our mission is to magnify God and to share the saving grace of Jesus Christ. (John 17:18, Mark 16:15)

Our destiny is settled. (John 14:1-3)

Our life is eternal and one day we will be in the presence of the Lord Jesus Christ forevermore. (Revelation 21:3-4)

Share His saving grace with everyone you meet.

2 *Remember Me - A Course in Rightly Remembering*, pages 60-63, The Will of the Testator.

The person God uses, is
quiet enough to hear Him,
brave enough to proclaim Him,
honest enough to obey Him.
— Vance Havner

Q. 19

How can I understand the Trinity?

The Doctrine of the Trinity is difficult to understand because our finite human brains are unable to fully conceive of an infinite being. However, God's Word gives us everything we need to come to an understanding of the nature of God as a Triune Being.

The Bible teaches that the Father is God, Jesus is God, and the Holy Spirit is God—and that there is only one God. Each Person of the Trinity is Himself distinct. We often simply state this as: The Trinity is one God, existing in three Persons (remember this does not mean three Gods. It means three distinct Persons, ONE God).

The word Trinity is not found in Scripture but the foundation for our doctrinal understanding and definition of it is most definitely found there. Trinity is understood to be synonymous with the term Triune God—three coexistent, co-eternal and co-equal Persons who are one God. Let's look at some scriptural references to better understand the Trinity.

There is one God

Deuteronomy 6:4 Hear, O Israel: The LORD our God is one LORD...

1 Corinthians 8:4 ...we know that an idol is nothing in the world, and that there is none other God but one.

Galatians 3:20 Now a mediator is not a mediator of one, but God is one.

1 Timothy 2:5 For there is one God, and one mediator between God and men, the man Christ Jesus...

The Trinity consists of three Persons

Genesis 1:1 In the beginning God created the heaven and the earth.(The Hebrew word for God used in Genesis 1:1 is Elohim, a plural word)

Genesis 1:26 And God said, Let ***<u>us</u>*** *make man in* ***our*** *image, after* ***our*** *likeness...*

Genesis 3:22 And the LORD God said, Behold, the man is become as ***<u>one of us</u>****, to know good and evil...*

Genesis 11:7 Go to, let ***<u>us</u>*** *go down...*

Isaiah 6:8 Also I heard the voice of the Lord, saying, Whom shall I send, and who will go for ***<u>us</u>****?*

Matthew 3:16-17 And ***<u>Jesus</u>****, when he was baptized, went up straightway out of the water: and, lo, the heavens were opened unto him, and he saw* ***<u>the Spirit of God</u>*** *descending like a dove, and lighting upon him: And lo* ***<u>a voice from heaven</u>****, saying, This is my beloved Son, in whom I am well pleased.* [In this verse we see the presence of all three Persons of the Trinity: the Son, Jesus, the Spirit descending and the Father speaking]

Matthew 28:19 Go ye therefore, and teach all nations, baptizing them ***<u>in the name</u>*** ***<u>of the Father, and of the Son, and of the Holy Ghost.</u>*** [Only one name, but three Persons]

2 Corinthians 13:14 The grace of ***<u>the Lord Jesus Christ</u>****, and the love of* ***<u>God</u>****, and the communion of* ***<u>the Holy Ghost,</u>*** *be with you all. Amen.* [Again we read of all three Persons of the Trinity]

1 John 5:7 For there are three that bear record in heaven, the ***<u>Father, the Word, and the Holy Ghost</u>****: and these three are one.*

Each Person of the Trinity is God. The Father is God (John 6:27, Romans 1:7, 1 Peter 1:2). The Son is God (John 1:1, John 1:14, Romans 9:5, Colossians 2:9, Hebrews 1:8, 1 John 5:20). The Holy Spirit is God (Acts 5:3-4, 1 Corinthians 3:16).

There is a pattern of subordination within the Trinity, regarding order, but not substance or essence. The Son is subordinate to the Father (Luke 22:42, John 5:36, John 20:21, 1 John 4:14); the Holy Spirit is subordinate to the Son and the Father (John 14:16, John 14:26, John 15:26, John 16:7, 13-14). We need to be careful to understand this subordination in terms of their work, not their Persons, power or position, for they are equal in those. Jesus surrenders to the will of the Father, or it could be said that He does the work that the Father gives Him to do:

> *John 17:4 I have glorified thee on the earth: I have finished the work which thou gavest me to do.*

The Spirit does the work of the Father and the Son:

> *John 16:7 Nevertheless I tell you the truth; It is expedient for you that I go away: for if I go not away, the Comforter will not come unto you; but if I depart, I will send him unto you.*

> *John 16:13-14 Howbeit when he, the Spirit of truth, is come, he will guide you into all truth: for he shall not speak of himself; but whatsoever he shall hear, that shall he speak: and he will show you things to come. He shall glorify me: for he shall receive of mine, and shall show it unto you.*

Yes, the Trinity is a difficult doctrine. While it can never be fully comprehended it can be understood by studying God's Word. And, just as we see the Trinity revealed in the Bible, we can also see triunity (the quality or state of being triune) in God's design.

Triunity is found everywhere in pattern: past, present and future; thought, word and deed; good, better and best; faith, hope and love; three Levitical feasts—Passover, Shavout and Tabernacles; three roles of Christ—Prophet, Priest, King; Three parts of our salvation—we are justified, sanctified, and we will be glorified.

As we clearly see God's pattern of triunity in the world around us, we see a pattern that reveals God's design. The Godhead is Father, Son and Holy Spirit and we are told that in Christ dwells the fullness of the Godhead bodily (Colossians 2:9).

To better understand the doctrine of the Trinity, undertake a study of the three Persons in the Godhead. Study their attributes and learn about their works. Always remember, there is only one God in all existence at all time (Isaiah 43:10; 44:6,8; 45:5) and in unity the three Persons of the Godhead work.

Who created the universe? The Father, Psalm 102:25; the Son, Colossians 1:16, John 1:1-3; the Spirit, Genesis 1:2 Job 26:13

Who created man? The Father, Genesis 2:7; the Son, Colossians 1:16; the Spirit, Job 33:4

Who brought about the incarnation? The Father, Hebrews 10:5; the Son, Philippians 2:7; the Spirit, Luke 1:35

Who brought about the crucifixion? The Father, Psalm 22, Romans 8:32, John 3:16; the Son, John 10:18, Galatians 2:20; the Spirit, Hebrews 9:14

Who brought about the atonement? The Father, Isaiah 53; the Son, Ephesians 5; the Spirit, Hebrews 9:14

Who brought about the resurrection? The Father, Acts 2:23, Romans 6:4; the Son, John 10:17-18, John 2:19; the Spirit, 1 Peter 3:18, Romans 8:11

Who brought about the resurrection of all mankind? The Father ,John 5:21; the Son, John 5:21; the Spirit, Romans 8:1

Who brought about the inspiration for writing of the Bible? The Father, 2 Timothy 3:16; the Son, John 1:1; the Spirit, 2 Peter 1:21

For there are three that bear record in heaven, the Father, the Word, and the Holy Ghost: and these three are one.
(1 John 5:7)

Q. 20

Can there be sin in Heaven?

Q. If there is no sin in Heaven, then why did Satan get cast out?

Let's begin with what we know from the words God spoke to the prophet Ezekiel found in Ezekiel 28:11-19. We know that Satan was created as an anointed cherub and was perfect until he rebelled against God (Ezekiel 28:15). He was then cast out of Heaven (Ezekiel 28:16).

When Satan rebelled, he took a third of the angels with him. So there were many angelic beings who exercised their free will and joined Satan in his rebellion against God. All rebellion against God is sin, so it's clear that there has been sin committed in Heaven. Often people will say that God cannot be in the presence of sin, but that statement is not biblically supported as indicated by the rebellion of Satan and the angelic beings.

It was pride that changed angels into devils; it is humility that makes men as angels. —St. Augustine

God is Sovereign over everything, and He is omniscient, omnipresent and omnipotent. In His omnipresence, He is everywhere. David said, *"If I ascend up into heaven, thou art there: if I make my bed in hell, behold, thou art there."* (Psalm 139:8)

Understanding that God is everywhere, we can understand that it is possible for Him to be in the presence of sin. Jesus in His incarnation was still God (fully God and fully man) and we know that He lived among sinners. Another case of sin being in God's presence in Heaven is found in Job 2:1

Again there was a day when the sons of God came to present themselves before the LORD, and Satan came also among them to present himself before the LORD.

It is possible for God to be in the presence of sin, but whether there is sin in Heaven at any time, we do not know. What we do know is that God will not permit any sin to go unjudged. He will justly judge all sin and impose its penalty.

Jesus' death on the cross paid the penalty for the sins of the world (John 1:29, John 3:16-18). He took the sins of the world upon Himself and His pure blood was shed to atone for our sins.

For those of us who have repented and trusted in Christ's finished work on the cross, our sins were judged at the cross of Jesus and paid for by Him. We have received forgiveness and have been washed clean by His blood. Christ's righteousness has been imputed to us and we are found to be clean and worthy because of what Christ has done for us.

For those who have not trusted in Christ, they have not received forgiveness of sins. All who die without forgiveness, and without having received Christ's righteousness, will be judged unworthy to enter into God's heavenly kingdom.

It should be our desire to share God's saving grace with everyone and to do as Jesus instructed Paul to do when He said to Paul that He was sending him to the Gentiles...

"to open their eyes, in order to turn them from darkness to light, and from the power of Satan to God, that they may receive forgiveness of sins and an inheritance among those who are sanctified by faith in Me." (Acts 26:18)

God is merciful and long-suffering. He desires that none should perish, but that all should come to repentance (2 Peter 3:9). Let's not be overly concerned with whether there could be sin in Heaven. Let's concern ourselves with the unrepentant sin on this earth and preach the gospel of saving grace to all—ourselves included.

Q. 21

If angels have free will to choose to obey God, does man [have free will] in Heaven?

When we repent and trust in Christ's finished work on the cross to pay for our sins, we are freed from the penalty of sin. We are also freed from the power of sin because Jesus conquered sin and death and has given us the presence and power of the Holy Spirit. However, while we remain on this earth, we live in an "already, but not yet" freedom. While Jesus conquered sin and death and gave us His Spirit to have power over sin, we all too often succumb to worldly and fleshly desires and sin. It will not be until we go to Heaven that we will be freed from the presence of sin.

The question presented asks if we will have free will once we are in Heaven and freed from the presence of sin. If the angels who sinned (2 Peter 2:4, Jude 6) were able to do so in Heaven, will we be able to do so? The underlying question here is, should we fear a second fall? Should we fear sinning in Heaven?

It's a good question because, IF (that's a hypothetical "if") man is able to sin in Heaven, then God would have to judge that sin and cast the person out from His presence, just as He did with the angels that sinned. That's a horrifying thought that we might lose our communion with the Lord. But the good news is...it's impossible for that to happen.

We know this because Christ promised that our new life in Him is eternal. His death on the cross paid the penalty for our sin and it is sufficient to both save us and keep us. We are His and we will be with Him forever. Nothing can separate us from Him.

*Jesus

Romans 8:35-39 Who shall separate us from the love of Christ? Shall tribulation, or distress, or persecution, or famine, or nakedness, or peril, or sword? As it is written, For thy sake we are killed all the day long; we are accounted as sheep for the slaughter. Nay, in all these things we are more than conquerors through him that loved us. For I am persuaded, that neither death, nor life, nor angels, nor principalities, nor powers, nor things present, nor things to come, Nor height, nor depth, nor any other creature, shall be able to separate us from the love of God, which is in Christ Jesus our Lord.

He has promised to never leave us or forsake us (Hebrews 13:5), so we can rest assured that we will never be separated from Him.

Tell me not, in mournful numbers,
Life is but an empty dream!—
Dust thou art, to dust returnest,
Was not spoken of the soul.
—Henry Wadsworth Longfellow

The question about whether man has free will in Heaven is not answered in Scripture. There isn't any Scripture to conclude that our free will is going to be taken away. However what is clear is that we will not sin because we are secure in our salvation, due entirely to the work of Jesus Christ. His righteousness has been imputed (credited) to us. It happened at the moment He saved us. It was a free gift, given by God and will never be taken away.

Jesus promised eternal life with Him—and eternal means eternal! So, our boasting throughout eternity will be praise of our great God for the righteousness of Christ that seals our souls eternally, from the penalty, power and presence of sin!

But God forbid that I should boast except in the cross of our Lord Jesus Christ, by whom the world has been crucified to me, and I to the world. Galatians 6:14 (NKJV)

Q. 22

Should we call His name Jesus? Or Yahweh? Or Yeshua?

Q. My friend (age 70) who is [denomination] by family line consistently brings up the fact that it makes him so angry when people call Yahweh "Jesus," because he says that the name Jesus was NEVER used in the Old Testament and that through generations of mankind it was man who named him Jesus. Therefore, we are wrong to use the name Jesus because it was NOT what God called Him. He said we need to properly call Him Yahweh or the other Hebrew names, but not Jesus. It makes my friend very angry. I tried to show him the New Testament Scripture where the angels called Him Jesus, but my friend does not believe this is true because the Bible has been rewritten so many times that the original Bible did not use the name of Jesus. How would you answer this kind of person?

Let's set aside your friend's skepticism about the reliability of the New Testament. That's another question for another day.

Your friend is not correct when he says that the name Jesus was not used in the Old Testament. But before I address that, let's begin with a foundational understanding that the Bible is progressive revelation.

We know that Yahweh (YHVH) is the covenant name of God that was revealed to Moses on Mt. Sinai prior to the exodus of God's people from Egypt. God appeared to Moses in a burning bush and Moses asked this question:

Exodus 3:13 Behold, when I come unto the children of Israel, and shall say unto them, The God of your fathers hath sent me unto you; and they shall say to me, What is his name? what shall I say unto them?

God answered Moses with these words:

Exodus 3:14 I AM THAT I AM: and he said, Thus shalt thou say unto the children of Israel, I AM hath sent me unto you.

Today, with the full revelation that we have in the Holy Scriptures, we understand the Great I AM to be a Triune God—one God in three distinct Persons: God the Father, God the Son and God the Holy Spirit. All three Persons are co-eternal, co-equal and coexistent in the one Godhead. So when God revealed His name of Yahweh to Moses, it was a revelation of the name of our Triune God. However, an Old Testament Israelite would not have understood God to be a Triune God. In fact the Shema proclaims *"God is one"* in Deuteronomy 6:4.

Hear, O Israel: The LORD our God is one LORD.

One Lord—that is precisely what God revealed to them, and exactly what He wanted them to understand at that time.

Next, remember that the Israelites were being prepared by God to recognize their coming Messiah, the "seed" promised in the Garden, who would rescue fallen man (Genesis 3:15). From the beginning in the Garden, and continuing throughout the Old Testament, we read of God revealing more and more of His purpose and plan of redemption.

When Jesus was born, the prophecy of a coming Messiah was fulfilled. When Jesus began His earthly ministry, He further revealed Himself as the promised Messiah. He also clearly claimed to be God. Regarding your friend's reasoning for not calling the Son by the name of Jesus, the Scripture clearly proclaims Jesus to be His name.

Matthew 1:21 And she shall bring forth a son, and thou shalt call his name JESUS: for he shall save his people from their sins.

To call the second person of the Trinity by the name Yahweh, rather than Jesus, fails to acknowledge an understanding of His incarnation and atoning work. Yes, Jesus is Yahweh and yes, our God is one God in three Persons. The name Jesus was given at the incarnation to the second Person of the Trinity when He came to live among us. It is a name that tells us of His mission and His works.

Peter made this very clear when he said:

Be it known unto you all, and to all the people of Israel, that by the name of Jesus Christ of Nazareth, whom ye crucified, whom God raised from the dead....Neither is there salvation in any other: for there is none other name under heaven given among men, whereby we must be saved. (Acts 4:10, 12)

Jesus is not a translation of the name Yahweh.

Jesus is actually an English name that derives from the Hebrew Yeshua (also Yehoshua or Joshua), which means God is Salvation. So while the Hebrew for the name Jesus is found in the Old Testament, it is not used in reference to God. Yahweh is the name of God in the Old Testament.

The etymology (study of the history of words, their origins, and how their form and meaning have changed over time) of the name Jesus is as follows:

The Hebrew/Aramaic name of Yeshua was translated as the Greek name Iesous. Then it was translated into Latin as Iesus. And from the Latin Iesus came the Anglicanized name of Jesus.

Yeshua or Jesus?

The names Yeshua (Hebrew) and Jesus (Anglicanized translation of Latin/Greek name) both refer to the second person of the

Trinity, so this raises another question. Is it more correct to use the Hebrew name Yeshua or the Anglicanized name of Jesus?

My answer is that either one is technically correct, because this is a matter of language not revelation. Both refer to Jesus of Nazareth. However, do both refer to our Saviour Jesus Christ? And, we should also ask, which name magnifies the Lord above all?

Yeshua is the name the Jews use to refer to the man Jesus of Nazareth. They believe him to have been nothing more than a good man and a prophet. Therefore the name Yeshua does not necessarily honor Jesus as Lord and Saviour.

If a Christian desires to use the Hebrew name, it would be good to include one of Jesus' titles so He is clearly identified as the Son of God. Yeshua Ha Mashiach is translated Jesus the Messiah. That leaves little doubt of His Lordship. And, Yeshua Ha Moshia is translated Jesus the Saviour. That clearly reveals He is the promised Redeemer.

In the English language, the name of Jesus is universally recognized as the name of our King (Messiah) and Saviour, but Christians might do well to use His full title....the Lord Jesus Christ.

Yeshua Ha Mashiach, Jesus the Messiah

Yeshua Ha Moshia, Jesus the Saviour

The Lord Jesus Christ

Whichever name you call Him...

To Him alone be the glory!

Q. 23

Do I need to be baptized like Jesus was baptized?

As we consider this, remember that the question asks, do I NEED to be baptized like Jesus was baptized. First, let's consider the possible reasons why Jesus was water baptized by John the Baptist.

There are some denominations that will say this baptism was a picture of what we must do for salvation. There are other denominations that will say a believer's baptism by immersion is an identification with Jesus' baptism. However, neither of these fit well with the biblical doctrine of salvation by grace ALONE, or with the baptism of Jesus by John.

> *Good works are indispensable to salvation—not as its ground or means, however, but as its consequence and evidence.*
>
> *—John R. W. Stott*

Water baptism does not save anyone. We can't do anything or add anything to Jesus' work in saving us (including getting baptized). Jesus saves sinners. He gets all the glory. It is only by His life, death, burial and resurrection that we can be made right with God and receive eternal life. It's not Jesus + my good works or Jesus + my good words. It's not Jesus + my Bible reading or Jesus + my church attendance. And it's also not Jesus + my baptism. It is always Jesus' work + nothing that offers salvation.

While water baptism does not have any part in saving us, it is a beautiful testimony to the grace and mercy we are given in salvation. It is by grace alone, through faith (Ephesians 2:8) in the finished work of Christ that we are saved.

Many churches proclaim water baptism to be a public outward profession of the personal inward change that has taken place in salvation. When Jesus saved us He cleansed us of sin and water baptism is a testimony to our being washed by the blood of Christ.

> *Revelation 1:5 And from Jesus Christ, who is the faithful witness, and the first begotten of the dead, and the prince of the kings of the earth. Unto him that loved us, and washed us from our sins in his own blood.*

So do we *need* to be immersed because Jesus was baptized that way? No. Then *should* we be immersed because Jesus was baptized that way? It depends. We all should desire to make a public profession of what Christ has done in saving us. In some churches that profession is made with water baptism and in others the profession is made in a sacrament called confirmation—a public statement of salvation in Christ.

What about Jesus' baptism by John?

There are denominations that claim by being baptized by full immersion in water we identify with Jesus in His baptism, but do we? If water baptism is a public proclamation that God has forgiven our sins, how does that identify with Jesus' baptism? Jesus' baptism did not in any way proclaim the forgiveness of sins. Jesus had no sins to be forgiven. Remember, John proclaimed Him as the Lamb of God who takes away the sin of the world (John 1:29). He was, is, and always will be the perfect, sinless Lamb of God.

> *Most men are notable for one conspicuous virtue or grace -- Moses for meekness, Job for patience, John for love. But in Jesus you find everything.*
>
> *—J. Oswald Sanders*

John preached a baptism of repentance for the remission of sins (Mark 1:4). He was baptizing *"with water unto repentance"* (Matthew 3:5). Jesus had no sins to repent of and therefore no need to be baptized "unto repentance."

We are baptized as a public profession of forgiven sins and an inward, spiritual rebirth. Jesus was not.

So why was Jesus baptized?

I will share with you what I have come to believe in my reading and studying of Scripture. I believe that Jesus was being consecrated for His public service for God and His ministry to the people. This was the practice for all priests who served in the Temple as God's ministers offering sacrifices. They were consecrated in a purification ceremony of being washed with water (Leviticus 8:6).

When Jesus came to John, and John hailed Him as *"the Lamb of God who takes away the sin of the world,"* Jesus was presenting Himself for His public ministry. There is no dispute that this was the beginning of Jesus' earthly ministry.

Just as with other priests, Jesus was consecrated by immersion in water, and we are told that He did this *"to fulfill all righteousness"* (Matthew 3:15). This baptism was a purification for service to God.

> *Matthew 3:16 And Jesus, when he was baptized, went up straightway out of the water...*

We then read of Jesus' being confirmed by the words of the Father, *"This is my beloved Son, in whom I am well pleased"* (Matthew 3:17, Mark 1:11, Luke 3:22) and empowered by the Holy Spirit, who descended upon Him like a dove (note: it wasn't a dove, it was *like* a dove).

We see the unity of the Trinity in Jesus' baptism. The Father, the Son and the Holy Spirit together. Remember, Jesus was 100% God and 100% man in His incarnation. Remember also that He and the Father and the Spirit are One God. They have never been, nor ever will be, separated. The Trinity is co-eternal, and yet, while here on earth, Jesus set aside His divinity, making Himself of no reputation (Philippians 2:7). He lived His life surrendered to the will of the Father and equipped for ministry by the power of the Holy Spirit.

Jesus' baptism was a whisper of His work on the cross.

Jesus' baptism is a beautiful picture of God's love for us. His baptism was not a public profession of forgiven sin (because He had none) but it does whisper of His coming death on the cross and His resurrection in victory over death and the sins of the world.

In the Bible, water consistently represents the judgment and wrath of God (the Flood – Genesis 6:17, Hebrews 11:7; the Red Sea drowning of the Egyptians – Exodus 14:28, Hebrews 11:29; Jonah going under the waters – Jonah 1, 2:3).

In His baptism, Jesus presented Himself and submitted Himself to go under the water as the Lamb of God. John proclaimed the work He would do…take away the sin of the world (John 1:29). In 3 1/2 years He would do the work of taking away the sin of the world. At the cross, Jesus was baptized again—this time immersed under the judgment of God. When Jesus took upon Himself the sins of the world and was nailed to the cross, God's wrath was poured out upon Him in righteous judgment of sin. His blood was shed to pay for our sins and then He gave up His life. He was buried and three days later rose from the grave victorious.

Jesus' baptism can be seen as a whisper, or a picture, pointing to the redemptive work that He would do at the end of His ministry, when He would offer Himself for the sins of mankind. Just as the Levitical system of sacrifice was a ministry of remission of sins, so also Jesus' baptism by John consecrated Him for His ministry of redemption of sin.

So when believers are baptized by immersion, I believe it more closely identifies with Jesus' work on the cross at Calvary, than with John's baptism of Jesus in the river Jordan. Our public profession of salvation should always focus on, "Jesus saved me." He went under the wrath of God (on the cross), so we would not have to go under that judgment. He paid the penalty for our sins so we would not face God's judgment and be condemned. Believers who go under the water in baptism do so as an identification with Jesus' death. We die to self and to sin, because Jesus died for us as a sacrifice to atone for our sin. We rise again to eternal life, not because Jesus came up out of the river Jordan, but because Jesus rose from the grave and conquered death.

It's all about Jesus! We are not washed by water, we are washed by His blood.

Please don't misunderstand me. I'm not saying that we should stop doing baptisms by immersion. Just remember to make it all about the One who did the work, the One who redeemed you. Let it be a public testimony to what Jesus has done for you. It's not about the believer getting baptized....it's about our Saviour and His mercy and grace in sacrificing Himself and restoring us to Himself.

It's always all about Jesus!!!

In my place condemned He stood;
Sealed my pardon with His blood.
Hallelujah! What a Savior!
(Man of Sorrows, What a Name)

We are the Bibles the world is reading; We are the creeds the world is needing; We are the sermons the world is heeding. —Billy Graham

Q. 24

Is a tattoo a poor testimony?

Q. Do you agree that the real reason to avoid tattoos is that it is a poor testimony to the eternal truth and urgency of biblical prophecy? Christians should avoid allowing any permanent mark to be made in or on his or her body as a reminder and a testament to the warning given in The Revelation of John. We are told that in the end times, people will accept the mark of the beast, and that will preclude salvation.

So is a tattoo a "poor testimony to eternal truth and urgency of biblical prophecy?" And, is not getting a tattoo "a reminder and a testament to the warning given in The Revelation?"

A Reminder

A reminder is something that brings to mind or causes someone to remember something. Usually a reminder is something seen, not the absence of something. However, I suppose an unmarked body could bring to *our own mind* the teaching that our bodies are temples of the Holy Spirit.

> *1 Corinthians 6:19...your body is the temple of the Holy Spirit who is in you, whom you have from God, and you are not your own?*

With the understanding that our bodies are temples of the Holy Spirit, we should also consider how we adorn our bodies (clothing, piercings, hair color and hair styles, makeup for women, etc). We should also consider how we present ourselves/our bodies (emotionally composed, kind and welcoming, versus angry, abusive, foul mouthed, etc). There's more than just tattoos to consider in adorning the *"temple of the Holy Spirit."*

All things are to be done to the glory of God, so a tattoo becomes a very personal and subjective decision that is needful of prayerful consideration before making a decisions to get one (or more). Always remember that we are called to represent Christ, so how we present ourselves is very important.

2 Corinthians 5:20 Now then we are ambassadors for Christ...

In answer to the question, an unmarked body could *possibly* be a reminder to oneself of future prophecy. But the same could be said about a tastefully done tattoo. A cross could be a reminder of God's love and grace. Again, this is truly a personal decision.

In trials of fact... the proper inquiry is not whether it is possible that the testimony may be false, but whether there is sufficient probability that it is true.
—Simon Greeneleaf

A Testimony

A testimony is defined as: a formal written or spoken statement, especially one given in a court of law. Since an unmarked body would be a testimony of silence, it really doesn't fit the definition, nor would it be very effective.

One might argue that having a tattoo can be a testimony. Although it is an unspoken testimony, people can read the tattoo or see and understand its message. A tattoo of a cross or other religious symbol, if done tastefully, could "speak" loudly to others. It could also be a means to opening conversations and sharing the gospel.

A friend of mine has a good example of a tattoo that can be used in this way. The tattoo features a cross with the letters VDMA and is tattooed on his arm. The four letters stand for the Latin words Verbum Domini

Manet in Aeternum, which translates as, The Word of the Lord Endures Forever. Those four Latin words were the motto of the Reformation. A tattoo such as this could make a culturally relevant and useful tool for evangelism.

To mark or not to mark? That is the question.

Always remember when considering a tattoo that Christians are to be a light to a lost and dying world. Therefore, we want people to find us welcoming by both our words and our appearance.

Matthew 5:14 Ye are the light of the world. A city that is set on an hill cannot be hid.

Do not judge by appearances. A rich heart may be under a poor coat.
—A Scottish Proverb

Tattoos do make a statement. Careful consideration should be given to what a tattoo "says" and to whom it "speaks." Also consider when it will "speak." By that I mean, what does it say about me and my beliefs today, and what will it say in five, ten, or more years? Tattoos are permanent and that should always be a major factor when considering getting one.

With Personal Liberty is Personal Responsibility

Christ has given us the gift of eternal life and a grace that says we are forever secure. Whatever we do, right or wrong, we will never earn more of His love or lose any of His love. He loves us!

We have liberty to live our lives, knowing that all of our sins were paid for by Christ and all of our sins are forgiven (past, present and future sins). With that freedom comes great responsibility—a responsibility to honor the One who gave His life for us.

There's no denying that some tattoos would be considered sinful by God and by some people. To make myself perfectly clear, I am speaking of those that glorify and present an unbiblical message, or have demonic subject matter. Anything that dishonors God is sinful. Never compromise and get a tattoo that does not honor God...even if it might be a way to open the door to speak with non-believers. Everything we do must always be God-honoring (Colossians 3:17).

Whether or not you should get a tattoo really depends more on the heart and the motive for getting it. Remember that Christ has given us His Spirit to lead and direct us. Therefore, we can trust that through the study of God's Word and through prayer His Spirit will lead and direct us in every decision we make.

Before getting a tattoo carefully discern your motives. Be honest with yourself. Remember, Christ already knows your heart...and tattoos are permanent.

Let your decision be rooted in love for Christ, gratitude for what He has done and guided by the Holy Spirit. Prayerfully make your decision.

Let's focus our eyes on Jesus and devote our hearts to him, and then let's go forth and preach the gospel ... with or without a tattoo.

Q. 25

Who is the twelfth apostle in Revelation 21:14?

And the wall of the city had twelve foundations, and on them were the twelve names of ***the twelve apostles*** *of the Lamb. (Revelation 21:14)*

Q. Why does this passage mention twelve apostles? Judas betrayed Jesus and he was one of the twelve. Can his name be written on the wall? I want to say that the twelfth name may be Stephen, but I am not sure. Could you please bring some clarification to this?

This is a most interesting question, and one for which there is not a definitive answer because the Bible doesn't tell us. Of course we know the identity of 11 of the apostles—and there certainly is agreement that Judas will *not* be the twelfth. Although the Bible does not tell us who the twelfth apostle is, by searching the Scriptures we can find information that presents two possible candidates.

Most Christians speculate that the twelfth apostle is either Matthias or Paul. Let's take a look at what we know about both men.

Matthias was chosen to be an apostle.

Acts 1:23-26 And they appointed two, Joseph called Barsabas, who was surnamed Justus, and Matthias. And they prayed, and said, Thou, Lord, which knowest the hearts of all men, show whether of these two thou hast chosen, That he may take part of this ministry and apostleship, from which Judas by transgression fell, that he might go to his own place. And they gave forth their lots; and the lot fell upon Matthias; and he was numbered with the eleven apostles.

Paul was called to be an apostle.

Romans 1:1 Paul, a servant of Jesus Christ, called to be an apostle, separated unto the gospel of God,

1 Corinthians 1:1 Paul, called to be an apostle of Jesus Christ through the will of God, and Sosthenes our brother,

2 Corinthians 1:1 Paul, an apostle of Jesus Christ by the will of God, and Timothy our brother, unto the church of God which is at Corinth, with all the saints which are in all Achaia:

Galatians 1:1 Paul, an apostle, (not of men, neither by man, but by Jesus Christ, and God the Father, who raised him from the dead;)

Ephesians 1:1 Paul, an apostle of Jesus Christ by the will of God, to the saints which are at Ephesus, and to the faithful in Christ Jesus:

Colossians 1:1 Paul, an apostle of Jesus Christ by the will of God, and Timotheus our brother,

1 Timothy 1:1 Paul, an apostle of Jesus Christ by the commandment of God our Saviour, and Lord Jesus Christ, which is our hope;

2 Timothy 1:1 Paul, an apostle of Jesus Christ by the will of God, according to the promise of life which is in Christ Jesus,

Titus 1:1 Paul, a servant of God, and an apostle of Jesus Christ, according to the faith of God's elect, and the acknowledging of the truth which is after godliness;

What requirements were necessary to be an apostle?

The word apostle means one who is sent, and it signifies an authorized representation to the point of having equivalent authority as the one who did the sending. In modern terms we might understand this position to be that of an ambassador, whose responsibility is to perform his work according to the will of the one who sent him, or to represent the sender in his absence, or to deliver the words of the sender.

We find in Scripture that both of these men, Matthias and Paul, were chosen and sent. We know from Scripture that Paul fulfilled his calling, but nothing more is mentioned about Matthias after his initial calling (Acts 1:23-26). However, just because Scripture is silent about Matthias does not give us reason to think that he did not fulfill his calling. Legend says that he served as a missionary to Ethiopia and was probably martyred there. But remember, that is not biblical...it is only legend.

An apostle had to be an eyewitness of the risen Christ.

Matthias witnessed the risen Christ. — *Acts 1:21-23 Wherefore of these men which have companied with us all the time that the Lord Jesus went in and out among us, Beginning from the baptism of John, unto that same day that he was taken up from us, must one be ordained to be a witness with us of his resurrection. And they appointed two, Joseph called Barsabas, who was surnamed Justus, and Matthias.*

Paul was a witness to the risen Christ. — *1 Corinthians 9:1-2 Am I not an apostle? am I not free? have I not seen Jesus Christ our Lord? are not ye my work in the Lord? If I be not an apostle unto* *others, yet doubtless I am to you: for the seal of mine apostleship are ye in the Lord.*

An apostle had to be chosen by God.

Matthias — *Acts 1:26 And they gave forth their lots; and the lot fell upon Matthias; and he was numbered with the eleven apostles.*

Acts 2:1 And when the day of Pentecost was fully come, they were all with one accord in one place.

Acts 2:4 And they were all filled with the Holy Ghost,

Paul — *Acts 9:15 But the Lord said to him, "Go, for he is a chosen vessel of Mine to bear My name before Gentiles, kings, and the children of Israel.*

An apostle possessed the God-given gifts to perform signs and wonders.

Matthias — *Acts 2:43 Then fear came upon every soul, and many wonders and signs were done through the apostles.*

Paul — *2 Corinthians 12:12 Truly the signs of an apostle were accomplished among you with all perseverance, in signs and wonders and mighty deeds.*

So is the twelfth apostle Matthias or Paul?

Again, we do not know. Scripture does not tell us. However, many believe that it will be Matthias because of the pattern of 12, which is a number that is directly related to Israel.

Matthias — The number twelve represents perfection and completion in relation to Israel. Consider the patterns in leadership, government, divine authority and appointment: 12 patriarchs, 12 tribes, 12 special anointings for government service, 12 disciples during Jesus' earthly ministry, 12 apostles sent at Pentecost, 12,000 from each of the 12 tribes) will be sealed and sent in the Tribulation, 12 foundations in the New Jerusalem (Revelation 21:14), 12 gates (Revelation 21:12, 21), 12 pearls (Revelation 21:21, 12 angels (Revelation 21:12), 12 legions of angels (Matthew 26:53), 12 thrones (Matthew 19:28), and more!

With the Judas' betrayal of Jesus and then his subsequent death, Peter proclaimed from Scripture (Acts 1:20, Psalm 109:8) that there must be 12 apostles and Jesus confirmed it (Matthew 19:28).

> *Acts 1:20 "For it is written in the book of Psalms*[*Psalm 109:8]*: 'Let his* [reference to Judas] *dwelling place be desolate, And let no one live in it'; and, 'Let another* [man appointed apostle] *take his* [Judas'] *office.'*
>
> **Psalm 109:8 Let his days be few; and let another take his office.*
>
> *Matthew 19:28 So Jesus said to them, "Assuredly I say to you, that in the regeneration, when the Son of Man sits on the throne of His glory, you who have followed Me will also sit on twelve thrones, judging the twelve tribes of Israel.*

Paul — Although there are many who think it could be Matthias, there are others who think it could be Paul because of the great work he did in spreading the gospel and building the church. However, Paul himself qualified that his apostleship was to the Gentiles (Romans 11:13, 1 Timothy 2:7, 2 Timothy 1:11).

Who knows?

Nobody really knows, but I lean toward it being Matthias. It seems much more likely that Matthias would be the twelfth because of the pattern of 12 in leadership and government of Israel and because Paul was the *"apostle to the Gentiles."* And, it seems likely that those whose name are on the foundations of New Jerusalem are the names of twelve who walked with Christ during His earthly ministry.

The twelfth name inscribed on the foundations of New Jerusalem has been discussed and debated for centuries. Remember, only God knows. I encourage you to do additional study and come to your own decision as to whether it might be Matthias or Paul.

Since the Scriptures do not tell us, we should all defer to the words of the prophets Jeremiah and Ezekiel, and others, who said....*Oh, Lord thou knowest!* Be comfortable with the mysteries that are in the Bible, knowing that God is in control and is working all things for our good and His glory.

Let us also remember that God promises that one day all things will come to pass, all prophecies will be fulfilled, and all mysteries will be revealed. One day there will be 12 names of apostles on the foundation of the wall of New Jerusalem, and we will know who the 12th one is. One day God's plan of restoration will be completely fulfilled. One day all things will be made new!

Oh what a glorious day that will be!

Q. 26

Revelation 22:17 speaks of the bride beckoning to "come." Who is the bride?

Revelation 22:17 And the Spirit and the bride say, Come. And let him that heareth say, Come. And let him that is athirst come. And whosoever will, let him take the water of life freely.

We should never read a Bible verse! To truly understand the meaning of any verse we should *always* look at verses in the broader context. Let's begin with chapter 22 verse 1 to better understand verse 17. The apostle John is recording what was shown to him, and what was told to him.

In Revelation 22 John records what was spoken by an angel and by Jesus. Revelation 21:9 tells us of this angel:

"there came unto me one of the seven angels which had the seven vials full of the seven last plagues, and talked with me, saying, Come hither, I will show thee the bride, the Lamb's wife."

The angel shows John New Jerusalem, God's new creation coming down from Heaven. In chapter 22 we read:

Revelation 22:1-6 And he [the angel] *showed me a pure river of water of life, clear as crystal, proceeding out of the throne of God and of the Lamb. In the midst of the street of it, and on either side of the river, was there the tree of life, which bare twelve manner of fruits, and yielded her fruit every month: and the leaves of the tree were for the healing of the nations. And there shall be no more curse: but the throne of God and of the Lamb shall be in it; and his servants shall serve him: And they shall see his face; and his name shall be in their foreheads. And there shall be no night there; and they need no candle, neither light of the sun; for the Lord God giveth them light: and they shall reign for ever and ever. And he said unto me, These sayings are faithful and true: and the Lord God of the holy prophets sent his angel to show unto his servants the things which must shortly be done.*

What a beautiful vision John saw and what a glorious description of what we will one day see. John continues to behold this beautiful vision...and then Jesus spoke to him, saying:

Revelation 22:7 Behold, I come quickly: blessed is he that keepeth the sayings of the prophecy of this book.

Jesus reminds John of His imminent return and the blessing for those who keep His Word. In verse 8 John reminds us that he SAW these things, and he HEARD them. He saw the glory of the new creation and He saw the glory of the Alpha and the Omega, the Great I AM, the Creator of everything—and he heard the words of His risen Lord and of the angel. It caused John to fall down and worship.

Revelation 22:8-9 And I John saw these things, and heard them. And when I had heard and seen, I fell down to worship before the feet of the angel which showed me these things. Then saith he unto me, See thou do it not: for I am thy fellowservant, and of thy brethren the prophets, and of them which keep the sayings of this book: worship God.

The angel reminded John that only God is worthy of worship. And then he told him *"the time is at hand"* and when that time comes the character of man will be revealed:

Revelation 22:10-11 And he saith unto me, Seal not the sayings of the prophecy of this book: for the time is at hand. He that is unjust, let him be unjust still: and he which is filthy, let him be filthy still: and he that is righteous, let him be righteous still: and he that is holy, let him be holy still.

Jesus then spoke again, proclaiming who He is and what He will do:

Revelation 22:12-13 And, behold, I come quickly; and my reward is with me, to give every man according as his work shall be. I am Alpha and Omega, the beginning and the end, the first and the last.

And the angel echoed the Lord's words:

Revelation 22:14-15 Blessed are they that do his commandments, that they may have right to the tree of life, and may enter in through the gates into the city. For without are dogs, and sorcerers, and whoremongers, and murderers, and idolaters, and whosoever loveth and maketh a lie.

Jesus confirmed that the angel is His messenger to the churches:

Revelation 22:16 I Jesus have sent mine angel to testify unto you these things in the churches. I am the root and the offspring of David, and the bright and morning star.

In verse 16 Jesus spoke of the local churches. The gathering of people, who come together for corporate worship. Now we come to the verse in question, who is the bride?

Revelation 22:17 And the Spirit and the bride say, Come. And let him that heareth say, Come. And let him that is athirst come. And whosoever will, let him take the water of life freely.

The bride is the body of Christ—all those who have repented of sin and trusted in Christ's life, death, burial and resurrection and have been redeemed by the blood of the Lamb.

It is not the corporate church, for we know that in every church gathering there are both believers and non-believers. It is the communal Church—all those who are in relationship with Jesus Christ, by the power of His Holy Spirit, who indwells all believers. And for that reason, it is the Spirit and the bride who then say, *"Come."* They're saying, "come" to the Saviour. And whoever thirsts will be satisfied by the Water of Life, the Living Water, the Lord Jesus Christ.

John saw a glimpse of eternity and He shared it with us. One day we will see what John saw. Do you invite people to come to the Saviour? Will you share your hope of glory with someone today? And what is that "hope of glory?" It is Christ in you!

To whom God would make known what is the riches of the glory of this mystery among the Gentiles; which is Christ in you, the hope of glory: (Colossians 1:27)

Q. 27

Why are there two different genealogies for Jesus?

Q. I was reading the genealogy of Jesus in Matthew 1 and Luke 3 and have two related questions.

First, although the genealogy is essentially the same at the end points (Adam/Abraham to Joseph), the genealogy is different in the middle (Matthew lists Solomon as the son of David, whereas Luke lists Nathan). At the end, Matthew lists Joseph as the son of Jacob, while Luke lists Joseph as the son of Heli. I am not sure how to reconcile those differences.

Second, both genealogies trace Jesus' lineage to David through Joseph, not Mary. But since Jesus does not have any earthly/blood linkage to Joseph, why is Jesus' lineage to Joseph important? Joseph is Jesus' father by adoption, so wouldn't Jesus' lineage to Mary be more important?

These are some of the most often asked questions by skeptics in their attempts to discredit the Bible. They believe these are contradictions and therefore proclaim them to be errors in the Bible. However, as we know, there are no errors in the Bible. There are answers for all these questions and explanations to dispel any doubt.

The Genealogies of Jesus Christ

Matthew and Luke record the legal and blood-line genealogies that give proof of the promises of Genesis 3:15. In the Garden, immediately following the fall of man, God promised to send a "seed"

*Jesus

who would rescue man from his fallen state. God spoke directly to the serpent Satan and said:

> *Genesis 3:15 And I will put enmity* [hostility/hatred] *between thee and the woman, and between thy seed and her seed; it* [the seed of the woman who is Jesus Christ] *shall bruise thy* [Satan's] *head, and thou* [Satan] *shalt bruise his* [the seed of the woman, Jesus Christ] *heel.*

From that time forward God began revealing His purpose and plan to His people:

With the birth of Jesus, God gave the world the promised Seed.

With the birth of Jesus, God gave the world Light and Hope.

With the birth of Jesus, God fulfilled His promise to send a Conquerer.

The genealogy of Jesus as recorded in Matthew.

Matthew's first verse proclaims Jesus' legal right as Messiah, the anointed one, a King who would come from the Tribe of Judah. The promised Seed was to come through Abraham (Genesis 22:18) and through David (Isaiah 11:1).

> *Matthew 1:1 The book of the generation of Jesus Christ, the son of David, the son of Abraham.*

Matthew next proceeds to record the line of succession. As correctly noted, when this genealogy reaches David, the succession proceeds through King Solomon. In contrast, in the book of Luke it proceeds with Nathan, the second surviving son of King David and Bathsheba.

Because Matthew is presenting Jesus as the coming Messiah to the nation of Israel, he provides a genealogy that begins with the father of the nation, Abraham, and the continues his record through King Solomon and all the way to Jesus' earthly father Joseph. This is the record of Jesus' genealogy through Joseph. It presents Jesus' legal right to the throne of David, to be Messiah (which means anointed One or King) from the Tribe of Judah.

The genealogy of Jesus as recorded in Luke.

The Gospel of Luke presents Jesus as the Son of Man and reveals Him in all His humanity to be 100% man. Luke begins with Joseph and traces the genealogy all the way back to the first man Adam. Luke 3:23 records Joseph as the son of Heli. In contrast, Matthew records Joseph as the son of Jacob. Is this an error?

> *Luke 3:23 And Jesus himself began to be about thirty years of age, being (as was supposed) the son of Joseph, which was the son of Heli...*

> *Matthew 1:16 And Jacob begat Joseph the husband of Mary, of whom was born Jesus, who is called Christ.*

Is this a contradiction? These are clearly two different genealogies for Joseph. Two different names are given for Joseph's father. In addition, reviewing the genealogy after King David, the Matthew account goes through King Solomon, the first surviving son of David and Bathsheba, but the Luke account goes through Nathan, their second surviving son. Nathan was never a king in Israel. Therefore, the Luke genealogy does not support Jesus' right to the throne of David. Nathan was, however, a son of David from the Tribe of Judah, so this genealogy does support Jesus as a son (descendant) of David.

Why two different genealogies for Jesus?

This is not a contradiction and the answer is really quite simple. Matthew is the genealogy of Jesus through Joseph and Luke is the genealogy of Jesus through Mary.

That raises the question, why does Luke record it as the genealogy of Joseph? It clearly lists Joseph, not Mary, in Luke 3:23.

To understand this requires some background about Jewish marriage and inheritance laws and customs.

Before proceeding, note that in Matthew we read each person was begotten ("begat" is used in KJV, "born" is used in modern translations). The word "begat" is defined as: to become the father of (someone) or to procreate as the father.[3] Notice that Matthew 1:16 does not say that Joseph "begat" Jesus, but rather that Jesus was "born" of Mary. The word "born" is defined as: brought into life by the process of birth.[4] This records that Jesus was not Joseph's biological child, but rather the child born of his wife Mary. This supports that Jesus was the adopted son of Joseph, not the begotten son. Of course we know that Jesus was begotten of God.

John 3:16 For God so loved the world, that He gave His only begotten Son, that whosoever believeth in Him should not perish, but have everlasting life.

Luke records the genealogy of Jesus through Mary.

Clearly this is not the bloodline of Joseph, for at King David it proceeds through David's son, Nathan. Again, this is Mary's genealogy. Heli was Mary's father and Joseph is listed in the text because he was the adopted son of Heli.

To understand this we must turn to the book of Numbers. Chapter 36 provides Jewish laws and customs regarding marriage and inheritance. In Numbers 36 we read about the distribution of the land among the children of Israel.

Numbers 36:1-2 And the chief fathers of the families of the children of Gilead, the son of Machir, the son of Manasseh, of the families of the sons of Joseph, came near, and spoke before Moses, and before the princes, the chief fathers of the children of Israel: And they said, The LORD commanded my lord to give the land for an inheritance by lot to the children of Israel: and my lord was

3 http://www.merriam-webster.com/dictionary/beget

4 http://www.merriam-webster.com/dictionary/born

commanded by the LORD to give the inheritance of Zelophehad our brother unto his daughters.

Zelophehad was of the generation of people who were not allowed entrance into the Promised Land and therefore died in the wilderness. We read in Numbers 27 of Zelophehad's five daughters who came before Moses, Eleazar the priest and the princes of all the congregation. They brought a petition to request an inheritance of their father's land as a way to preserve his name. Inheritance was always through the male line, so the daughters asked,

Numbers 27:4 Why should the name of our father be done away from among his family, because he hath no son? Give unto us therefore a possession among the brethren of our father.

Moses responded exactly as we should respond in all matters. He *"brought their cause before the LORD."* (Numbers 27:5) And the Lord answered Moses:

Numbers 27:7 The daughters of Zelophehad speak right: thou shalt surely give them a possession of an inheritance among their father's brethren; and thou shalt cause the inheritance of their father to pass unto them.

There was however a provision required so the name and lineage of the father would be preserved. The daughters were to marry within their own tribe (Numbers 36:6-9) so the land would remain in the tribe of their father.

Heli was Mary's father. Without any sons, Heli adopted Joseph as his son for the purposes of inheritance, by the provision of God recorded in the book of Numbers. Both Mary and Joseph were from the Tribe of Judah, and therefore Mary met the requirement of marrying within the same tribe.

Finally, let's read Luke 3:23 again and consider what it says:

And Jesus himself began to be about thirty years of age, being (as was supposed) the son of Joseph, which was the son of Heli.

The word "supposed" in this verse is the Greek word nomizo and means: to do by law, to accustom, to deem or to regard. So we understand this to mean that Joseph was "reckoned by law," not by birth, as a son to Heli.

In summary:

1.There is a Torah exception on rules of inheritance.
 It was requested by Moses on behalf of the daughters of Zelophehad (Numbers 27:1-5).
 It was granted by God (Numbers 27:6-11).
 It was defined by God (Numbers 36:6-9).
 It was instituted by Joshua (Joshua 17:3-6).

2. Mary met the required provision when she married within her tribe (Matthew 1:16).

3. Joseph was the adopted son of Heli, reckoned by law (Luke 3:23).

4. Matthew records the genealogy of Jesus, through Joseph. Matthew records from Abraham to Joseph, Jesus' legal right to the Throne of David as the Messiah of Israel.

5. Luke records the genealogy of Jesus, through Mary. Luke starts with Mary (although Joseph's name is listed) and traces the genealogy all the way back to Adam. This provides Jesus' birthright and bloodline as the Son of Man.

We now understand why the genealogies differ in their beginnings (Abraham and Adam) and after King David (Solomon and Nathan), and why two different names are given for Joseph's father. At Christmas we celebrate the birth of Jesus, the Son of God, the son of Mary and the adopted son of Joseph.

Christmas is a remembrance of the past—God's gift of Jesus, an assurance for the present—His grace is sufficient, and a hope for the future — He will make all things new. May your cup overflow with God's blessings and your path be directed by His light.

Q. 28

Didn't God proclaim a blood curse on Jesus' ancestors? What's the explanation for this?

Having addressed the supposed contradiction in the two genealogies of Jesus as recorded in Matthew and Luke, this raised a question about the blood curse of Jeconiah as recorded in Jeremiah.

The Blood Curse of Jeconiah

Jeconiah was a wicked king and God decreed that none of his descendants would ever ascend to the throne of David.

> *Jeremiah 22:30 Thus saith the LORD, Write ye this man* [Jeconiah] *childless, a man that shall not prosper in his days: for no man of his seed shall prosper, sitting upon the throne of David, and ruling any more in Judah.*

Jeconiah was a descendant in the line of Solomon, so the genealogy in Matthew is tainted with a blood curse, beginning with Jeconiah and continuing all the way to Joseph. No blood descendant of Jeconiah would ever be acceptable to God as King of Israel.

This does not, however, disqualify Jesus since Joseph was only his legal father, not his biological father. Jesus was the legal son/descendant of Joseph, but not by blood. Therefore Jesus was not of the seed of Jeconiah. Jesus did not have Joseph's blood, and therefore the blood curse was not passed on to him.

> *Good news from heaven the angels bring; Glad tidings to the earth they sing: To us this day a child is given, To crown us with the joy of Heaven. — Martin Luther*

The only blind person at Christmas is he who has not Christmas in his heart.
— Helen Keller

Mary was Jesus' only human parent. It was through her ancestry that Jesus had a birthright in the bloodline of the Tribe of Judah, from which all kings came. The genealogy of Jesus through Mary is not through Solomon but through Nathan (the second surviving son of King David and Bathsheba). Jeconiah was not an ancestor of Mary's and therefore no blood curse was upon her descendants.

If (and that's a hypothetical "if") Joseph had been Jesus' biological father, Jesus could *not* have fulfilled the prophecy of being King of Israel.

Joseph was not Jesus' biological father, but Mary was His biological mother. That supports the virgin birth, which is exactly what was prophesied:

> *Isaiah 7:14 Therefore he Lord himself shall give you a sign; Behold, a virgin shall conceive, and bear a son, and shall call his name Immanuel.*

> *Matthew 1:23 Behold, a virgin shall be with child, and shall bring forth a son, and they shall call his name Emmanuel, which being interpreted is, God with us.*

> *Luke 1:35 And the angel answered and said to her, "The Holy Spirit will come upon you, and the power of the Highest will overshadow you; therefore, also, that Holy One who is to be born will be called the Son of God."*

As early as the second century, the church affirmed this very simply and clearly in The Apostle's Creed:

> *"I believe ... in Jesus Christ, his only Son, our Lord, who was conceived by the Holy Spirit, born of the Virgin Mary...."*

The Nicene Creed (325, 391 AD) further defines the implications of the virgin birth with greater clarity:

> *"We believe ... in one Lord Jesus Christ, the only-begotten Son of God, begotten of the Father before all worlds, Light of Light, very God of very God, begotten, not made, being of one substance with the Father...."*

For the Christ-child who came is the Master of all; No palace too great, no cottage too small. — Phillips Brooks

In summary, Joseph was Jesus' earthly, adopted father. God is Jesus' heavenly Father. Jesus was begotten of God, conceived by the Holy Spirit. Mary was Jesus' human mother, a young virgin who gave birth to the Son of God. The blood curse upon Joseph's line was not passed on to Jesus. Mary's blood line was pure in that it was without the blemish of a curse. Jesus' blood was pure when He went to the cross, for He never sinned. The Lord Jesus Christ fulfilled the prophecy of the Lamb of God, pure and spotless, who took away the sins of the world (John 1:29).

Jesus is by all accounts the
King of king
and
Lord of lords.

Thanks be to God for his unspeakable gift.
2 Corinthians 9:15

Behold, a virgin shall be with child, and shall bring forth a son, and they shall call his name Emmanuel, which being interpreted is, ***God with us.***

— Matthew 1:23

Q. 29

Are there genealogies of Jesus recorded in Mark and John?

We've addressed the supposed contradiction in the two genealogies of Jesus in Matthew and Luke; and we've looked at the blood curse of Jeconiah found in the genealogy recorded in Matthew. But what about the Gospels of Mark and John? Do they contain genealogies?

Many Bible readers believe that only the Gospels of Matthew and Luke record genealogies for Jesus. However, that is not the case. Each of the Gospels, in its own way, offers a genealogy. Let's first review how Matthew and Luke present the genealogies.

The Genealogies of Jesus in Matthew and Luke

Matthew presents Jesus as the legal heir to the throne of David and gives the genealogy from Abraham to Joseph. Matthew reveals the promised Messiah, the coming King, the Lion of the Tribe of Judah. Jesus is presented in His royalty.

Luke presents Jesus' birthright as a man born of Mary. Although Joseph is listed, the genealogy found in Luke is Mary's lineage. Luke records the genealogy of Joseph all the way back to the first man Adam. He presents Jesus in His humanity as the Son of Man and a son of David born of the Tribe of Judah.

So, if Matthew and Luke record genealogies, what about Mark and John? Most people think those Gospels don't record a genealogy. While that is true of Mark, it is not of John.

The Genealogy of Jesus as Recorded in John

John presents Jesus as the Son of God, revealing Him in all His divinity to be 100% God.

The genealogy of Jesus found in the book of John is presented in the first verse. It is very short in words, but very long in time. It begins with Jesus, the Word, and traces his lineage all the way back to the beginning. It is the genealogy of the preexistent One who is from eternity past and it provides Jesus' rightful claim of divinity. John reveals Jesus as the Son of God, who is One with the Father.

John 1:1-2 In the beginning was the Word, and the Word was with God, and the Word was God. The same was in the beginning with God.

The Genealogy of Jesus in Mark?

It is correct to note that the book of Mark does not present a genealogy of Jesus. This raises the question, why would it be omitted? The other three Gospels record 1) Jesus' legal right to the throne as the Messiah, 2) His birthright to the throne as the Son of Man, a son of David from the Tribe of Judah, and 3) His divine right as the Son of God because He IS God! So why no genealogy in Mark?

The book of Mark presents Jesus as a suffering servant, who came in humility and obedience to the will of His Father.

Mark 10:45 For even the Son of man came not to be ministered unto, but to minister, and to give his life a ransom for many.

No pain, no palm; no thorns, no throne; no gall, no glory; no cross, no crown.
— *William Penn*

The genealogy of a servant or slave was not noteworthy of record and therefore no genealogy is recorded in Mark. The book of Mark does not focus on the Lord's teachings, parables or revelations of divine truth, but rather it illuminates the Lord's ministering works.

The book presents great pictures of the Lord's works. It's almost like reading a script for a play with the actions so clearly chronicled and with the most glorious of endings. The "curtain falls" on the book of Mark with a wonderful visual of the Lord ascending to Heaven and his followers going forth into the world to serve Him.

> *Mark 16:19-20 So then, after the Lord had spoken to them, He was received up into heaven, and sat down at the right hand of God. And they went out and preached everywhere, the Lord working with them and confirming the word through the accompanying signs. Amen.*

Special Revelation in Each Gospel

His royalty: Matthew presents Jesus as the Messiah, the coming King. Jesus' genealogy is recorded from Abraham to Joseph, making Jesus a legal heir to the throne of David.

His humility: Mark presents Jesus as the Suffering Servant, prophesied in Isaiah, of whom there is no genealogy provided because a slave's genealogy was not worthy of record.

His humanity: Luke presents Jesus as the Son of Man, a messianic title from the prophecy of Daniel, and as a son of David, a title used frequently to denote His lineage from the Tribe of Judah. This genealogy begins with Joseph, as the husband of Mary, and traces Jesus' ancestry through Mary's bloodline all the way back to the first man, Adam.

His divinity: John presents Jesus as the Son of God, the second person of the Trinity. Jesus' genealogy is recorded as the eternal God, coexisting with God the Father from everlasting.

All of this was prophesied and fulfilled in the birth of Jesus:

> *But thou, Bethlehem Ephratah, though thou be little* [Mark's humble servant] *among the thousands of Judah* [Luke's Son of Man from the Tribe of Judah], *yet out of thee shall he come forth unto me that is to be ruler in Israel* [Matthew's coming King]; *whose goings forth have been from of old, from everlasting* [John's Son of God].
>
> *Micah 5:2*

A readiness to believe every promise implicitly,
to obey every command unhesitatingly,
to stand perfect and complete in all the will of God,
is the only true spirit of Bible study.
— Andrew Murray

Q. 30

What makes the Bible so unique?

The Bible is made up of 66 books written over 1,500 years and penned by about 40 different writers—most of whom did not know each other. The writers came from many different backgrounds, with varying status, economic and educational levels. The writers wrote in various geographic locations and with differing circumstances and emotions. The Bible was written on three different continents (Asia, Africa and Europe) and in three different languages (Hebrew, Aramaic and Greek).

The Bible is unique from all books in that it was divinely given through humans. It was penned by human writers, in human language, recording human history and revealing a fully human man.

- The Bible is divine in that it records the Word of God, given by God, and it reveals a divine Saviour who came to rescue sinners.
- The Bible is God-breathed and written *through* man rather than written *by* man.
- The Bible provides all the answers to all questions, especially those that are of utmost importance to all mankind:

Who is God?

Who is man?

Why am I here?

What is wrong with the world and man?

How can things be made right?

The unity of the Bible is due to the fact that it has one author, God. The Bible reveals one Triune God in three persons—Father, Son and Holy Spirit—and it reveals one Redeemer, the Lord Jesus Christ. The Bible begins with Jesus and ends with Jesus; and on every page the Bible is a testimony to His Person and His works. We do not worship the Bible. We worship the person whom the Bible reveals, the Lord Jesus Christ.

The clarity of the Bible is evidence of God's ability and desire to be in communion with His creation. It is simple enough for a child to read and deep and rich enough for the most learned of scholars. The Bible is inexhaustible in knowledge and wisdom. It imparts an understanding of God's mercy for the sinner and His grace to all who will come to Christ. It can be read by people from all walks of life, in all countries and languages.

The Bible is the only book that provides an absolute standard of truth and defines morality and ethics based on a solid foundation that is not subject to change. It is concise and consistent. It is inerrant, inspired and infallible. It contains prophecies that have been perfectly fulfilled, and others that are yet to be fulfilled. It provides all knowledge for man's understanding of God, the world and the times.

The Bible—A Gift from God to Us

The modern world detests authority but worships relevance. Our Christian conviction is that the Bible has both authority and relevance, and that the secret of both is Jesus Christ.

— John R. W. Stott

Throughout history many have recognized the great gift of God's Word and proclaimed their daily need for the Bible to strengthen and sustain them and to grow and deepen their relationship with their Saviour.

The book of Hebrews speaks of a "*great cloud of witnesses*" (Hebrews 12:1), those who have walked before us in faith, and continue to inspire and encourage us by their faith.

> *Hebrews 12:1 Wherefore seeing we also are compassed about with so great* ***a cloud of witnesses****, let us lay aside every weight, and the sin which doth so easily beset us, and let us run with patience the race...*

A Cloud of Witnesses

Hebrews 12:1 speaks of the Old Testament saints as a great cloud of witnesses to those alive at the time. While they continue to be a witness and testimony to us through the pages of Scripture, in our times we also have a "cloud of witnesses" who encourage us to remember the importance of God's Word in our lives.

The Holy Scriptures are our letters from home. — Saint Augustine

A thorough knowledge of the Bible is worth more than a college education. — Theodore Roosevelt

Take all that you can of this book upon reason, and the balance on faith, and you will live and die a happier man. — Abraham Lincoln
[Response when a skeptic expressed surprise seeing Lincoln reading a Bible]

As Commander-in-Chief I take pleasure in commending the reading of the Bible to all who serve in the armed forces of the United States. Throughout the centuries men of many faiths and diverse origins have found in the Sacred Book words of wisdom, counsel and inspiration. It is a fountain of strength and now, as always, an aid in attaining the highest aspirations of the human soul.

— Franklin D. Roosevelt, January 25, 1941

[Letter from the White House to the Armed Forces on the first page of my father's military-issued New Testament and Psalms pocket Bible.]

Within the covers of the Bible are the answers for all the problems men face. — Ronald Reagan

We can never learn too much of His will towards us, too much of His messages and His advice. The Bible is His word and its study gives at once the foundation for our faith and an inspiration to battle onward in the fight against the tempter. — John D. Rockefeller

Unless we form the habit of going to the Bible in bright moments as well as in trouble, we cannot fully respond to its consolations because we lack equilibrium between light and darkness. — Helen Keller

The Bible will keep you from sin, or sin will keep you from the Bible. — Dwight L. Moody

The Bible was not given for our information but for our transformation. — Dwight L. Moody

A Bible that's falling apart usually belongs to someone who isn't.
— Charles H. Spurgeon

The Bible is worth all the other books that have ever been printed.
— Patrick Henry

I study my Bible like I gather apples. I search the Bible as a whole like shaking the whole tree. Then I shake every limb - study book after book. Then I shake every branch, giving attention to the chapters. Then I shake every twig, or a careful study of the paragraphs and sentences and words and their meanings. — Martin Luther

The Word of God well understood and religiously obeyed is the shortest route to spiritual perfection. And we must not select a few favorite passages to the exclusion of others. Nothing less than a whole Bible can make a whole Christian. — A. W. Tozer

All miseries and evils that men suffer from—vice, crime, ambition, injustice, oppression, slavery and war—proceed from their despising or neglecting the precepts contained in the Bible. — Noah Webster

Word of God Speak

In addition to the voice of the "cloud of witnesses" who have gone before us, the Word of God itself speaks to us. The Bible empowers, equips and encourages us in our daily walk in faith with the Lord.

John 1:1, 14 In the beginning was the Word, and the Word was with God, and the Word was God. John 1:14 And the Word was made flesh, and dwelt among us, (and we beheld his glory, the glory as of the only begotten of the Father,) full of grace and truth.

Romans 15:4 For whatever things were written before were written for our learning, that we through the patience and comfort of the Scriptures might have hope.

2 Timothy 2:15 Study to show thyself approved unto God, a workman that needeth not to be ashamed, rightly dividing the word of truth.

2 Peter 1:5 And beside this, giving all diligence, add to your faith virtue; and to virtue knowledge;

Psalm 119:89 For ever, O LORD, thy word is settled in heaven.

Matthew 24:35 Heaven and earth shall pass away, but my words shall not pass away.

I hope in thy word.

Psalm 119:81, 114

WE HAVE THIS
HOPE
AS AN ANCHOR FOR THE SOUL
A HOPE BOTH
SURE AND
STEADFAST.

HEBREWS 6:19

About the Anchor on the Cover

In my book, *Why the Butterfly? Rightly Remembering Jesus* and the companion study course, *Remember Me*, I focused extensively on three significant changes that take place when we **rightly remember who God is, what He has done for us and who we are in Christ**. When we filter all that we think, say and do through rightly remembering Jesus it changes our perspective and our priorities and guides our thoughts, words and actions.

Rightly remembering Jesus will...

1) Establish your heart

2) Anchor your soul

3) Transform your mind

Our hearts are established with Christ's grace. (Hebrews 13:9)
Our souls are anchored with Christ's hope. (Hebrews 6:19)
Our minds are transformed with the word of His Power.
(Romans 12:1-2, Hebrews 1:3)

The Hebrews 6:19 verse that supports the anchoring of the soul has long been a very special one for me:

This hope we have as an anchor of the soul, both sure and steadfast...

*Jesus

I know what it is like to feel adrift in a sea of sadness and despair and it was truly hope in the Lord that kept my "boat" safe and above water. His grace, His hope and His power kept me in the "boat," safe from "drowning."

It's little surprise to me that God in His loving kindness moved me into the ministry of Reasons for Hope*Jesus. Our ministry logo proclaims hope in the Lord with an asterisk that leads to the name above all names.

reasonsfor**hope***

***Jesus**
our only true hope!

When I shared with my friend and graphic designer Tamara Schmitz, my idea to use an anchor on the cover, she designed what you see on the front of this book. She also shared with me something of great interest that I did not know—the anchor was a symbol of Christianity in the early church.

As we know, an anchor for a ship or boat provides stability and safety in both calm and dangerous weather by holding the ship in one place. In storms, when the waters are tumultuous, the winds are violently strong and the rains are torrential, the anchor prevents the ship from being tossed and turned by tethering it to the bottom of the sea or ocean. In calmer weather and waters the anchor keeps the ship from drifting.

How very similar is our hope in Christ. When the world's temptations, trials and tribulations rock our "ship," our stability is anchored in Christ and is without tossing, turning or drifting. Christ provides the real safety and security that gives us peace and hope.

The anchor ranks as one of the earliest Christian symbols and was used on many tombstones and epitaphs as an indication that the deceased had died "in Christ." It served as a testimony to belief in the hope and promise of resurrection from the dead.

The anchor was also a symbol of security and hope for those oppressed in various reigns of terror and was known to be the symbol of St. Clement of Rome, who tradition says was martyred when he was tied to an anchor and thrown into the sea.

For early Christians facing persecution, an anchor could easily evoke thoughts of the Apostles, most of whom were sea-faring fishermen, and most of whom were persecuted and died for their faith. Again, an anchor symbolizes that Christ is the true stability in the storms of life and that His cross alone opens the way to forgiveness of sin and the hope of navigating the sea of life until that day when we reach our home shores in Heaven.

Like the early Christian symbol of a fish, an anchor is quite simple to draw. Considered to be a Chrismon—a Christian symbol representing Jesus Christ—the drawing of an anchor has been thought to incorporate a stylized form of Alpha and Omega shown in lower case Greek letters and transformed into the symbol.

AΩ = αω =

Of course, we can easily recognize the representation of the cross in the symbol of an anchor, as well as a circle that represents wholeness.

Next time you see an anchor, whether real or a symbol, you might just look at it a little differently. Let it call to remembrance the hope you have in Jesus, the salvation you have now and eternally with Him and the promise of your final rest from all the storms—for He truly is the Anchor in this sea of life!

His Sufficient Grace

By Shari Abbott

May the mind of Christ live in me,
Every minute of every day.
May the grace that He has given me,
Establish my heart in His perfect way.
(Hebrews 13:9)

May I always reflect that wondrous love,
His sacrificial gift.
That others, in me, might also see,
His Light, His Joy, my Hope.

May the hope that flows from only Him,
Anchor my soul, steadfast and strong.
(Hebrews 6:19)
So when the storms of life arise
He is my strength, my song.

In the face of all adversity,
In Him I'll find my rest.
His promise is to comfort me,
In that, I know I'm blessed.

May my mind be ever transformed by Him,
Surrendered to His Word and will.
(Romans 12:1-2)
For He's given me the Power I need,
(Hebrews 1:3)
His strength that does fulfill.

His Spirit now lives in me,
Assuring, I never am alone.
He's with me now, and forever will be,
My new and perfect home.

May I rest always in Jesus Christ,
the One and only Son.
Who's given me a redeeming love,
A grace that says it's done.

I shall remember His will and ways,
Sufficient grace He's given me.
I'll follow Him, all my days,
'Til my journey's end I see.

And then one day, to my delight,
I'll go to be with Him.
I'll see Him in His glory bright,
My Saviour, my reigning King.

Now may the God of hope fill you with all joy and peace in believing, that you may abound in hope by the power of the Holy Spirit. (Romans 15:13)

Books & Resources from this Author

Who Said That? Common Everyday Sayings
This is a great book to give to unbelievers. It's simply a look at everyday sayings originating from God's Word. At the end of the book is a gospel presentation.

A Room with a View of Eternity—The Last Will & Testament of the Lord Jesus Christ
Take a seat at the Master's table. Learn about the Lord's final words to His faithful disciples (John 13-17), and the riches He gives to all who are His. This book will bless and encourage you, provide you with hope, and help you live in the joy of your salvation.

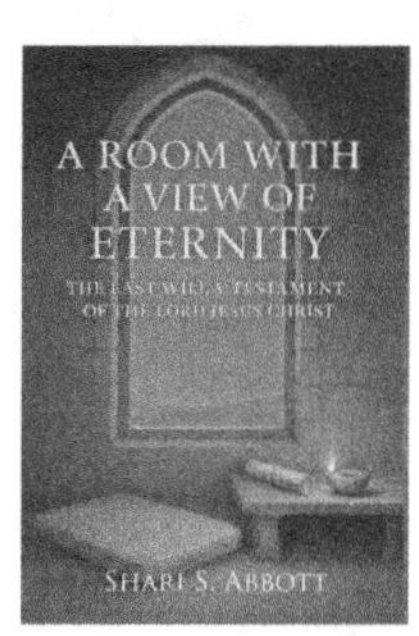

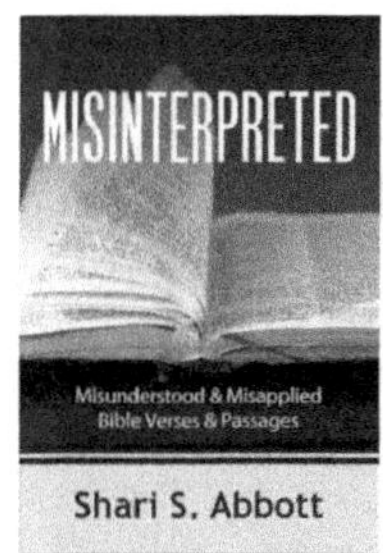

MISINTERPRETED - Misunderstood & Misapplied Bible Verses & Passages—Sometimes Scripture is wrongly taught with an intention to deceive, but most often it is unintentional. As Christians, we must be diligent in discerning truth —God's truth from His Word.

Got Questions? We have Reasons for Hope
Reasons Books 1, 2, 3 & 4

Real questions from real people. Each book has 30 questions and 30 answers with reasons for hope.

Why the Butterfly? Rightly Remembering Jesus—This book isn't about butterflies. . .it's all about Jesus! Discover how rightly remembering will establish your heart, anchor your soul, and transform your mind. A quick read that will give you a heavenly perspective on this journey we call life!

Remember Me - A Course About Rightly Remembering

Seven video study sessions that teach rightly remembering and will ignite in you a desire to filter everything you think, say and do through the hope that is found in Jesus Christ. Learn how *rightly remembering* will establish your heart, anchor your soul, and transform your mind.

Fun with Shuns Learn the key doctrines of the Christian faith by understanding the many words in the Bible that end in "-tion". The study includes five short videos. If you can't fully explain why you believe what you believe, then you need this study. DVD and book for group or individual study.

Hear, See, Speak No Evil—Plus a Fourth Monkey The three little monkeys, with their proverbial quip, "Hear No Evil, See No Evil, and Speak No Evil," date back as far as 17th century. What biblical lessons do these monkeys offer? And what about the newest warning. . .post no evil?

How to Witness to Jehovah's Witnesses, Apologetics Answers & Verses Get prepared to defend what you believe and be able to present biblical truth the next time a Jehovah's Witness comes to your door. Don't be out-witnessed by a Jehovah's Witness.

Quotable Quotes - Words Worth Remembering — s a treasury of timeless wisdom from Christian voices across the ages. Carefully chosen quotations are paired with Scripture references to encourage you to delve deeper into the biblical truths that relate to the insightful quotes..

Forty Names of Jesus for Forty Days of Lent — A daily devotional companion inviting you to slow down, open God's Word, and fix your heart on Jesus by reflecting on one of His many names and titles. Allow the Holy Spirit to deepen your love for "The Risen Christ," your Shepherd, Savior, and King.

*Rightly Dividing the Word of Truth —*With simple explanations and Scripture-centered teaching, you'll discover how a right understanding of Scripture brings clarity instead of confusion, confidence instead of doubt, and joy as you see how every part of the Bible fits together in God's perfect plan. This is your invitation to become a faithful workman—*rightly dividing the Word of Truth.*

This hope we have as an anchor for the soul, both sure and steadfast. (Hebrews 6:19)

Helping Christians to know Jesus better, by

Offering biblical answers and reasoning from God's Word, and

Promoting the benefits and joys of spending time with God in prayer and in reading and studying His Word, which leads to

Enjoying God, finding rest in Jesus, and living to honor Him and serve others.

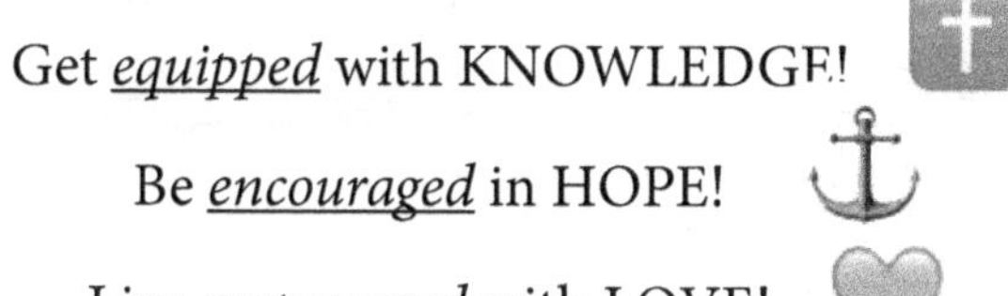

About Reasons for Hope* Jesus

Our ministry exists to glorify God by equipping Christians with biblical knowledge, understanding, and wisdom. Knowing and trusting God and growing in understanding of His will and ways will change our world. Jesus is the Reason this Ministry Exists, but YOU make it possible!

If Reasons for Hope* Jesus has blessed you, please consider supporting our ministry. Your goodwill and generosity makes possible our mission to equip, encourage, and empower the body of Christ and reach the lost with the gospel of saving grace. www.reasonsforhopeJesus.com/donate.

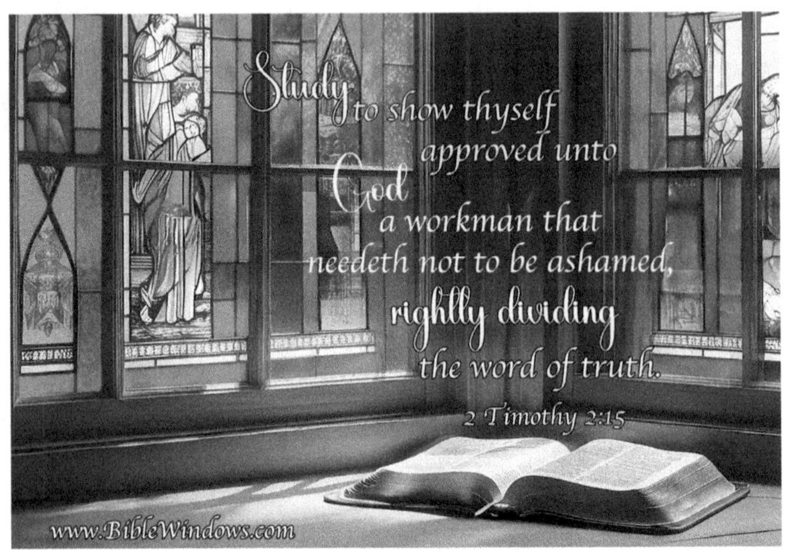

Visit www.BibleWindows.com
for all our song videos and
Bible teachings videos

Questions?

Email us at questions@reasonsforhopeJesus.com

Contact Us

Email us at hope@reasonsforhopeJesus.com

Connect With Us

www.reasonsforhopeJesus.com

www.biblewindows.com

Facebook: www.facebook.com/reasonsforhopeJesus/

Twitter: www.twitter.com/reasons4hope

YouTube: www.youtube.com/reasonsforhopeJesus

Visit the Store

www.reasonsforhopeJesus.com/store

Sign Up

At www.reasonsforhopeJesus.com for apologetics teachings and biblical encouragement with true hope and real joy.

May the God of hope fill you with all joy and peace in believing, that you may abound in hope by the power of the Holy Spirit. Romans 15:13

Have Hope!

Now hope does not disappoint, because the love of God has been poured out in our hearts by the Holy Spirit who was given to us.

—Romans 5:5

Be Bold!

Therefore, since we have such hope, we use great boldness of speech;

—2 Corinthians 3:12

[Praying] for me, that utterance may be given to me, that I may open my mouth boldly to make known the mystery of the gospel, for which I am an ambassador in chains; that in it I may speak boldly, as I ought to speak.

—Ephesians 6:19-20

Share the Gospel

Since we have the same spirit of faith, according to what is written, "I believed and therefore I spoke," we also believe and therefore speak.

—2 Corinthians 4:13

As it is written: "How beautiful are the feet of those who preach the gospel of peace, Who bring glad tidings of good things!"

—Romans 10:15

www.ingramcontent.com/pod-product-compliance
Lightning Source LLC
LaVergne TN
LVHW010914110826
845149LV00013B/2354

* 9 7 8 0 9 8 8 5 5 1 3 4 3 *